So When Does the Fat Lady Sing?

So When Does the Fat Lady Sing?

*Questions and
Answers about Life,
Sex, Love, and–
Oh, Yes–Opera*

by Michael Walsh
Introduction by Placido Domingo

𝄞
AMADEUS
PRESS

An Imprint of Hal Leonard Corporation
New York

Published in 2007 by Amadeus Press
An Imprint of Hal Leonard Corporation
19 West 21st Street, New York, NY 10010

Printed in the United States of America

Book design by Stephen Ramirez

Library of Congress Cataloging-in-Publication Data is available upon request.
ISBN-10: 1-57467-162-6, ISBN-13: 978-1-57467-162-9

With the exception of the following, all photographs are by Henry Grossman.

Photographs on pp. iii, vi, xiii, xix, 1, 55 and 113 are courtesy of Photofest. Photographs on pp. 1, 55 and 113 are by Louis Mélançon, Metropolitan Opera.

The photograph on p. iii (title page) is of Kirsten Flagstad as Brünnhilde in *Die Walküre.*

www.amadeuspress.com

For Stephanie von Buchau (1939–2006): opera lover,
gourmet, baseball fan and dear friend

Maria Callas in *Tosca*

CONTENTS

Introduction

Opera is my life. It has been since I was growing
up in Mexico, watching my parents perform
in *zarzuela* and dreaming that someday I, too,
would be up there on the stage, singing.

Little did I suspect how my dream would turn out.
Today I can proudly say that I have sung every major
tenor role in the repertoire at opera houses around the
world. Lately, I've conducted many of them as well. But
all this operatic activity has only whetted my appetite
for more. As Shakespeare said, "Age cannot wither her,
nor custom stale, her infinite variety," and I would like to
think the Bard of Avon could have had opera in mind.
(If only opera had been flourishing then! What librettos
Shakespeare might have given us!) You can spend a lifetime in opera, and still not know the half of it.

That's why even I have been stumped by some of the questions you'll find in this volume. What my old friend Michael Walsh—for 16 years the music critic of *Time* magazine—has done (and, yes, critics and performers can become friends, strange as it may seem) is to put opera into an entirely new context. Michael and I first met 25 years ago in San Francisco—on a baseball field, playing for opposing teams—and in this book he's still playing hardball. There's some soft-tossing, more than a few curves and, every once in a while, just to keep you honest, a high hard one over the middle of the plate.

Have you ever stopped to consider which operas might today be called "politically incorrect"? Or in which operas the principal characters don't sing at all? Or which operas are based on the lives of real people? You'll find the answers within.

But you'll also find much more, including a witty and informative history of opera, neatly divided into three acts, which forms the heart of the book. You'll also be quizzed on the subtitles of the Gilbert and Sullivan operettas, asked to identify the literary origins of some famous operas and even given a short course in the wit and wisdom of George Bernard Shaw. Ever wonder how Hollywood might pitch some famous operas? The answers are here.

Whether you're an expert or a beginner, there's something here for everyone. You can learn from scratch, or brush up on your Schoenberg and your Schubert. Or just sit back and have a rollicking good time.

Now let's see . . . who was that Louisiana-born composer whose contributions to one of the most popular operas ever written make him, by far, the most-performed American composer of all time? Hmmmm . . .

—*Placido Domingo*

Three images of Placido Domingo in his signature role, Otello. *Can you identify the evil Iago in this Metropolitan Opera production of Verdi's masterpiece? And on which Mediterranean island does the tragic story of these two men unfold? Turn the page for the answer.*

Placido Domingo surprised many opera cognoscenti when he rolled the dice and added the part of Lohengrin to his repertoire. Is this opera the first or last of Richard Wagner's Ring des Nibelungen *cycle? Find the answer on the opposite page.*

Answers: Introduction Photo Captions

1 James Morris, Cyprus.

2 Neither—nor.

Opposite: Enrico Caruso in *Rigoletto*

Prologue: *Sí Puo?*

So you think you know opera, eh? Oh, sure, you can rattle off the names of the great divas of the past hundred years, laugh at the obscure jokes in funny foreign languages, parse a few of the plots, and, from the safety of your record and CD collections, mayhaps even provide an all-time dream-cast list. Maybe you can answer all the questions on the weekly Metropolitan Opera radio quiz, just like the bona fide bigdomes they get on the program. Maybe you've even been on the quiz. But does that really make you an opera expert?

That's what we're here to find out. There are plenty of Q&A books out there that purport to try your operatic mettle, to assay your operatic IQ and to put your knowledge of operatic lore to the test. But if you ask me, they're all kid's stuff. Trivia for the cognoscenti; interrogatory fillips for the jaded. What we're after here is the World's Most Operatic Opera Quiz—because this is a quiz about opera. Not about singers, opera houses, productions or gossip. In short, it's about the music and the composers.

What a concept! For too long, opera lovers who care more about the opera than who's singing it have been made to feel like second-class citizens in their own opera houses. "Did you enjoy Signor Testosterone's Cavaradossi?" "Well, my dear, it was not a patch on Luigi Buonasera's legendary painter that I heard him sing while he was having the affair with Madame Puttanesca in Buenos Aires in 1954!" That sort of thing.

Instead, we're after something deeper and richer: via the Socratic method, we're here to learn more about an art form we already love—or want to learn to love—within the overall cultural context that has nourished it for several hundred years. Call it the World's Most Useful Opera Quiz.

In other words, this is a book for both the tyro and the connoisseur. For the neophyte, it provides a brief *tour d'horizon* of operatic history over the past four centuries, and can be read exactly that way. Don't worry about keeping score: just read the interrogatory dialogue as if you were overhearing two people talking about opera. Leap about, jump ahead, read all the subquizes whenever you want: hey, it's your book!

For the expert, I've tried to challenge you by going beyond the realm of plot, character, dialogue and cast that is the usual purview of an opera-quiz book. Sure, you'll find some of that. But your knowledge of the wider world beyond opera will be probed as well. Name the operas. Under what circumstances were they written? How do the works of Composer X relate (sometimes in very odd ways) to the works of Composer Z? Get ready, get set—and get on your toes.

One way to learn about opera (besides actually attending one!) is to read a book on the subject, and there are plenty of good ones—including *Who's Afraid of Opera?* by yours truly. Every year, it seems, another couple of how-to and what-about books on opera issue forth from the publishers, throwing down the gauntlet to initiates and beginners alike. Some offer an opera-by-opera guide to the art form, rather in the manner of *The Daily Racing Form* or a fight card. Others take a broader, more philosophical approach, waxing wroth on the subject of *verismo, bel canto, gesamtkunstwerke* and other such foreign mysteries. Some are more practical, furnishing helpful guides to the best opera recordings of all time, in which an interested party ought to be investing his or her hard-earned money; others—given the speed at which new recording technologies come along—eschew that format as intrinsically dated and opt for a more general survey of the field.

What this book aims to do, however, is something completely different. Constructed in the time-honored operatic form of three acts, a prologue and an epilogue, it seeks to guide you, Virgil-like, through the labyrinths and lairs of the fabulous operatic beast. We'll survey primarily the art form itself—the *Ding an sich,* as Kant might say, if he had had a sense of humor—but we'll also throw in some queries concerning its ancillary manifestations, such as its venues, its practitioners and its lore, whether factual or apocryphal, which have sprung up around it over the four-centuries-plus that opera's been around.

In fact, you've already had your first question. Or, rather, your first three. Here they are again, in case you missed them:

Name three operas referred to in the paragraph just above.

Or, to make it simpler at this early stage,

1 Name the most famous opera constructed in three acts with a prologue and an epilogue.

2 Name an opera based on an epic poem by Virgil.

3 Name an opera that features a fabulous beast ensconced in a dark and dangerous lair.

And, while we're at it, for bonus points:

4 Name the opera referred to in the subtitle of this prologue.

There! That's wasn't so hard, was it? And what have we learned so far, quizmeisters and students alike?

That an operatic reference or analog can be found for nearly every human situation.

What I mean by that is simply this: opera, more than any other art form except perhaps the novel, is the truest reflection of the human condition yet devised by the mind of man. For man is an allusive animal; he seeks to explain the world—indeed, the cosmos—to himself by means of signs, symbols and references. Whether it is the ancients gazing at the stars and discerning Cassiopeia lurking within a random constellation, or Jerry Seinfeld finding crypto-fascism in a New York City soup joint, we love symbols so much that, in many ways, they are superior to the real thing. The murder of an errant wife and her young, virile lover by an aging husband in real life, is just more tabloid fodder in the Age of O.J. But in opera it's—

5 Well, what is it?

Yessirreebob, that's exactly what it is. And written a full century before a certain double homicide in Brentwood. And not just of *Pagliacci*, either, but of dozens of other operas that treat the Eternal Triangle and its operatically inevitable fatal consequences. So, just for fun, let's name a couple more:

Il Tabarro, by Giacomo Puccini.
(Jealous husband kills lover, and displays corpse to wife as curtain falls.)

Cavalleria Rusticana, by Pietro Mascagni.
(Jealous husband Alfio kills former and current lover, Turiddu, of his wife Lola, much to the chagrin of Turiddu's current spouse, Santuzza—not to mention his kindly old Mamma Lucia.)

Are you beginning to get the idea?

Don't worry: we're not here to intimidate you. Nothing puts off the opera wannabe faster than encountering a group of insiders, furiously one-upping each other by summoning up the most extreme arcana, put forth with an "only-a-complete-moron-doesn't-know-this" attitude. (The question usually has something to do with who sang the role of the Second Armed Man in the Metropolitan Opera's 1950-something production of *The Magic Flute*, or who made her U.S. debut as Die Amme in *Die Frau ohne Schatten* in San Francisco.) I mean, it's enough to turn one into an oenophile. If that's not illegal in your state!

Instead, we're here to test—and improve—your knowledge of opera. What it's about. Why it works. And sometimes why it doesn't. How music and text function within its structure. And, finally, what effect opera has on us, the listeners.

To that end, the questions contained herein will pop up naturally in the text and in the photo captions, as if you and I are having a conversation about opera. Some of them will have only one answer, others will have a number of correct responses. You will think of some answers that I haven't—and you will be right; some questions may have dozens of answers, but to save us both time and trouble, I've listed only a representative sampling. (That's the fun of opera: nobody is the ultimate expert.) A few questions may have no answers at all, but are designed to get you—and keep you—thinking about opera long after you've finished the book. Because unlike with most exams, when you're finished with this one you'll know a lot more about the subject than you did when you started. And you'll want to know even more. The only grades you'll get here are the ones you give yourself, and you'll know you've passed the course when you find yourself eagerly seeking out new operatic experiences. And isn't that the best kind of quiz?

Ladies and gentlemen, the orchestra is tuning up. Let's take our seats!

Answers: Prologue

1 *The Tales of Hoffman*, by Jacques Offenbach.

2 *Les Troyens*, by Hector Berlioz.

3 *Siegfried*, by Richard Wagner.

4 *I Pagliacci*, by Ruggero Leoncavallo.

5 It's the plot of *Pagliacci*!

So When Does the Fat Lady Sing?

Opposite: Lucia Popp in *Die Zauberflöte*

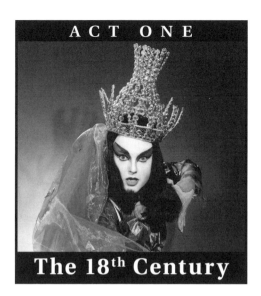

ACT ONE

The 18ᵗʰ Century

Mozart & Salieri

S trictly speaking, opera did not begin with Mozart.
But it came pretty close. Although opera was
invented in the late 16th century, the roots of the
modern repertory extend back only to the late 18th
century. So we'll begin where the standard repertory
does, with the great works of Mozart—which is where
anyone interested in opera would be likely to begin
anyway—and branch out from there.

For our purpose here is to illustrate just what makes
opera tick and how Mozart pretty much defined what the
ticking was all about. How it's put together, and why. Like
everything else we cherish in this life, from St. Peter's to
Moby Dick to Marilyn Monroe, opera is about structure,

structure, structure. Every successful work of art owes much of its success to a perfectly balanced internal and (sometimes, in the case of buildings) external architecture, which both frames and supports the ideas and emotions contained within.

But first:

1 Who wrote the first opera?

2 Where?

3 When?

4 What was it called?

5 Who wrote the libretto?

6 What was the occasion?

As opera evolved from the royal courts of Italy, hopped over the Alps to Austria and Germany and eventually swept the Continent, England and Russia, it needed one supreme creative artist to universalize it. To create a form, as it were, that would not only suit composers of many different nationalities, but would stand the test of time. Mozart was just the guy for the job. There were many who came before him, and far more who came after him. But none better.

7 Name at least eight important opera composers before Mozart and the works for which they are best remembered.

And now, without further ado, on to Amadeus!

8 Just what was Mozart's real name, anyway?

9 Did he ever call himself "Amadeus"?

10 So where does "Amadeus" come from?

11 What's the German version of Mozart's middle name?

12 And what does it mean?

13 And was it appropriate?

Everybody knows the broad outlines of Mozart's life—child prodigy, performer at the royal courts of Europe, victim of deep personal tragedy and, finally, sent to the grave at (to us) a premature age. But Mozart's life has also been the subject of so much myth and legend that it's hard to separate the fact from the fancy.

Let's start with the biggest myth of all—that he was murdered.

14 Was Mozart murdered?

15 If so, by whom?

16 Well, didn't they hate each other?

17 Where did the story get started, then?

18 So Peter Shaffer didn't make it up?

19 Which famous composer wrote an opera called Mozart and Salieri?

20 Which famous poet unwittingly contributed the libretto?

21 How many characters are in it?

22 Is Mozart a tenor or a baritone?

23 How is it?

24 Why don't we hear it more often?

25 Name some of Salieri's operas.

26 In 1786, "Prima la musica" was performed on a double bill with a Mozart work. Name the opera and the crowned head who enjoyed the show.

27 As long as we're on the subject of Mozart's rivals, who wrote *Belmonte und Konatanze, oder Die Entführung aus dem Serail* two years after Mozart did?

28 Why?

29 Is it true that listening to Mozart can cure headaches?

The hagiography began almost upon Mozart's death. As did the outpouring of grief, money, etc., that nowadays are *de rigueur* whenever a celebrity dies. (Why didn't they do or say that while the poor fella was alive?) Now that he was gone, everybody wanted to show how discerning he or she had been beforehand, how much they appreciated

Mozart's genius and how dearly the world was going to miss him. (Hypocritical, perhaps, but true). Writers immediately began collecting reminiscences of the great man and interviewing surviving family members, resulting in many myths about Mozart's life and times.

30 Name the early Mozart biographers, and describe how one or more of them was related to his or her subject.

31 Was Mozart buried in a pauper's grave?

32 Was there a fierce snowstorm at Mozart's funeral that prevented the mourners from accompanying the body to the cemetery?

33 Why do people make up stories like this?

34 Name another composer, born in the 18th century, whose death received some quasi-cinematic embellishing.

The point is that even the lives of the composers are sometimes the stuff that fantasy is made of: as they worked, according to this theory, so did they live.

Our age is less sentimental than the 19th century, the heyday of the great musical hagiographies. We prefer a more mechanistic approach to understanding our geniuses, perhaps in the hope that if we push all the same buttons, we can turn out to be just like them. Or better yet, they can turn out to be just like us. How else to account for those TV shows in which some huckster offers to sell you (the chump) his "ten great secrets for making money now!"?

35 What is his main secret?

In just the same way, we feel that if we understand that Mozart had an emotionally abusive father, along with a somewhat unhealthy attachment to his mother and a downright incestuous relationship with a female cousin—well, that just proves that even a so-called genius has feet of clay like the rest of us, doesn't it? We might call this defining genius down, and it seems to make us happy.

It is true that details of composers' lives can sometimes offer valuable clues into the kind of work they produced. And it's just as true that sometimes these details have nothing whatsoever to do with the work itself. Let's keep this in mind as we take our idiosyncratic look at Mozart and 18th-century opera in general.

Mozart lived in an age of royal courts and crowned heads. At the same time, the most important event of his lifetime was the American Revolution in 1776—

36 How old was Mozart at the time?

—which was followed a few years later by the French Revolution, which was still raging when he died. The periwigged Mozart still had to use the servants' entrance, but the fires of revolution nevertheless found their way into his music. And, in so doing, gave birth to the first—and some would say, still the greatest—of modern operas.

Do you recognize this distinguished gentleman? He is in costume for a production of Werner Henze's opera Der junge Lord *at the New York City Opera. Even though he appeared in only a single performance during his career he spends many nights at the opera. He himself claims over 5,000 nights. Got it? For more hints look at pages 21–22.*

37 What is this opera's name in Italian? In English? In German? In French?

38 And what's so great about it?

I'm assuming you either already know the answer to that question or you're here to learn. For if, by common consent, Mozart wrote four indisputable masterpieces, which remain in the repertory of every opera house in the world to this day—

39 What are they?

—the favorite pastime of Mozart lovers everywhere is debating the merits of each one, and trying to decide which is *primus inter pares*.

The opera in question, of course, is *Le nozze di Figaro*, which was based on the play by Beaumarchais, a French playwright whose ear was very much attuned to the martial music that was sweeping his country in the late 18th century.

40 What was Beaumarchais' given name, and what were some of his other occupations?

People today often think that sequels are a creature of Hollywood. But sequels can be found in the highfalutin', rarefied atmosphere of grand opera as well. In fact, *Figaro* is a sequel to an earlier Beaumarchais play, *Le barbier de Seville*.

41 Which famous 19th-century composer wrote the "prequel" to *Le nozze*?

What is it called?

What possessed his mother to name him "Giocchino"?

Beaumarchais went on to write a third play about his characters, which has been set by at least two 20th-century composers. One of them was more or less a complete flop and is rarely revived. The other was a *succes d'estime* on which the historical jury, however, is still out.

42 Name the play and the two composers who have written operas based on it.

43 Name the other operas these two composers have written.

Now let's get to the good stuff. Beyond the political significance of *Figaro* lies an old-fashioned good time in the theater, laden with heaping doses of mistaken identities, characters hiding in closets and leaping out windows and general hanky-panky. With the possible exception of the Countess, everyone in *Figaro* seems to be jumping around like a cricket.

44 Why?

45 Is opera always like this?

46 Why?

47 Does that mean that opera is harmful to children and other living things?

48 Are there any operas that are not somehow about sex?

49 Wasn't Mozart's librettist at least partly responsible for this shocking state of affairs? You know, what's-his-name?

50 In fact, wasn't he a dirty old man?

51 He wound up where?

Let's take the four great Mozart operas and see what they're all about.

First up is *Figaro*, and here is its plot: Count Almaviva wants to revive the ancient custom of the *droit de siegneur*, which would allow him to sleep with Susanna on the night of her wedding to his valet, Figaro—who, it turns out, is the illegitimate son of two of the opera's other main characters.

So, before we go any further:

52 What's Figaro's real name?

53 Who are his parents?

54 Whom does the Count desire?

55 Whom does Cherubino desire?

56 Whom does Figaro desire?

57 Whom does the Countess desire?

58 Whom does Barbarina desire?

(continued on page 16)

Books into Operas

Librettists and composers don't always think up their plots on their own. Many great (and some not-so-great) operas derive from pre-existing literary sources. Name the operas adapted from these famous novels, plays, poems or legends:

1 *Ivanhoe*, by Sir Walter Scott.

2 *Romeo and Juliet*, by Shakespeare.

3 *Billy Budd, Foretopman*, by Herman Melville.

4 *Henderson, the Rain King*, by Saul Bellow.

5 *Erdgeist* and *Die Büchse der Pandora*, by Frank Wedekind.

6 *War and Peace*, by Leo Tolstoy.

7 *Tom Jones*, by Henry Fielding.

8 *The Scarlet Letter*, by Nathaniel Hawthorne.

9 *The Lady of the Lake*, by Sir Walter Scott.

10 *Wuthering Heights*, by Emily Brontë.

11 *Die Leiden des jungen Werthers*, by Goethe.

12 *El Sombrero des tres picos*, by Pedro de Alarcón.

13 *King Lear*, by Shakespeare.

14 *The Little Foxes*, by Lillian Hellman.

15 *The Merry Wives of Windsor*, by Shakespeare.

16 *The Turn of the Screw*, by Henry James.

17 *Sumidagawa*, by Juro Motomasa.

18 *The Fall of the House of Usher*, by Edgar Allan Poe.

19 *Memoirs from the House of the Dead*, by Dostoyevsky.

20 *Paradise Lost*, by John Milton.

Politically Incorrect

With all its hot-blooded tenors, villainous baritones and blushing sopranos, opera is a veritable feast of stereotyping, as the following examples demonstrate:

1 In which opera does an Indian squaw make an appearance, and what is her name?

2 This repertory opera, a favorite with children, features a black character who's portrayed as a slobbering sex fiend.

3 In another opera, a black character is a slick-dressing, jive-talking pimp.

4 In this classic, the hero's hot-bloodedness is ascribed to his South American Indian parentage.

5 This beloved opera features not one but two heroines who are basically cheap, trampy, man-hunting gold-diggers.

6 Miscegenation, and the dim view taken of it by all concerned except the lovers, forms the basis of this opera's plot.

7 Child molestation, anyone?

8 In this repertoire staple, the hero's temper is attributed to his Basque forebears.

9 This gay character is portrayed as a dumb, suffering victim who finally dies, spurned and mocked, by the callous object of her affection.

10 A hunchback is kicked around like a clown in this classic, which never gives the handicapped an even break, much less a preferential parking space.

Probably the ultimate opera scene here with Teresa Stratas and José Carreras. Two arias, "Che gelida manina" and "Mi chiamano Mimi," followed by the duet "O suave fanciulla." You only have to come up with the name of the opera and composer. Find the answers on page 53.

(continued from page 10)

In *Così fan tutte*, two young men attempt to seduce each other's girlfriend after they make a playful wager with an old roué. Each of them succeeds, much to his own distress.

Don Giovanni is self-explanatory.

Meanwhile, *The Magic Flute* concerns itself with (among other things) Tamino's wooing of Pamina; the conflict between the good Sarastro and the evil Queen of the Night; the Moor Monostatos's attempted rape of Pamina and the extremely fecund pairing of Papageno and Papagena.

Did Mozart have sex on the brain? You bet! Mozart's letters to his mother and his female cousin are rife with obscenity, scatology, sexual innuendo and *double entendre*. As Maynard Solomon has pointed out in his magisterial biography, *Mozart*, there seems little question that Mozart enjoyed the physical favors of his cousin. Let's take a look at some of the women in Mozart's life, and talk about his family in general:

59 What was Mozart's mother's name?

60 What was Mozart's sister's name?

61 What was Mozart's cousin's name? What was her pet name?

62 What, did they run out of names?

63 How many siblings did Mozart have?

64 Did Mozart talk dirty?

65 And did he write dirty music, too?

66 Why, if he was such a great composer, did he act this way?

67 Were all the great composers as lusty as Mozart?

The point is that many of the great composers were highly sexually motivated, in a way that might get them arrested in our politically correct, neofascist-Puritan times. Or at least have some radical feminist seriously question their sanity in a series of Op-Ed pieces for the *New York Times.*

As his operas illustrate, Mozart was also wrapped up in the biggest political social issues of his day. We've seen how *Figaro* is a thinly veiled reference to the coming French Revolution—"sire, the peasants are revolting!"— but in another important aspect of his life, Mozart was on the front lines of his society.

68 Of which secret society was Mozart a member?

69 Who accounted for the society's fascination with ancient Egypt?

70 Who else, and what was he to Mozart?

71 How many Mozart operas are set in Egypt?

72 Which Mozart librettist was also a lodge brother?

73 Of which ethnic group is Tamino ostensibly a member?

74 How old is Papagena? Papageno?

75 Who is the good guy and who is the bad guy in *The Magic Flute*?

76 Does this make any sense?

77 Then why does it work?

78 How many people did Mozart know?

On the face of it, *The Magic Flute* is absurd. In this regard, it is not alone. Before Mozart, absurd or unbelievable librettos abounded (which is one reason why those operas are rarely performed today). It might amuse opera buffs to list some of the hundreds of opera composers between Monteverdi and Mozart who enjoyed a brief vogue with their operas about randy gods, goddesses, ancient Greek heroes and Roman tribunes, and now have vanished from memory, but why waste our time? We're here to talk about sterner stuff.

79 Well, how about naming some of the composers, then, just to see if we've heard of any of them?

80 Enough, already!

81 Is there anybody I have heard of?

82 On the other hand . . . I thought opera quiz books were supposed to test our knowledge of all sorts of recondite arcana. How come you seem to be stuck on Mozart?

Not the, but a Rosenkavalier. If you do not recognize him in five seconds, your reputation as an opera lover is forever damaged. Find the answer on page 53.

What Mozart did—the way he transformed opera from "an exotic and irrational entertainment"—

83 Wait a minute! I've heard that one before! Who said that?

84 You call that witty?

85 What has he got to do with a discussion of opera? I thought he wrote the dictionary. (Or was that Daniel Webster?)

86 Which were?

87 What was Handel's problem?

88 How fast a composer was Handel?

89 Did Handel's operas have something to do with, er, a delicate operation on young boys?

90 What were those singers called?

91 Who was the most famous of them all during Handel's time?

92 Weren't there a couple of rival female sopranos around that time, too?

(continued on page 25)

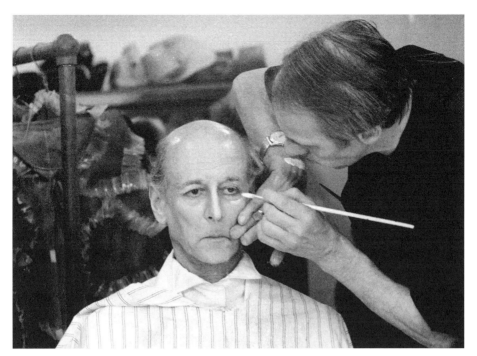

Have you already identified the legendary member of opera's nobility who is preparing for the only performance of his life?

On the stage of "his" opera house he greeted all kinds of performers, beauties and beasts, from Maria Callas to Ahmed the camel in a very realistic setting of Aida. Still no clue? Turn the page for further information.

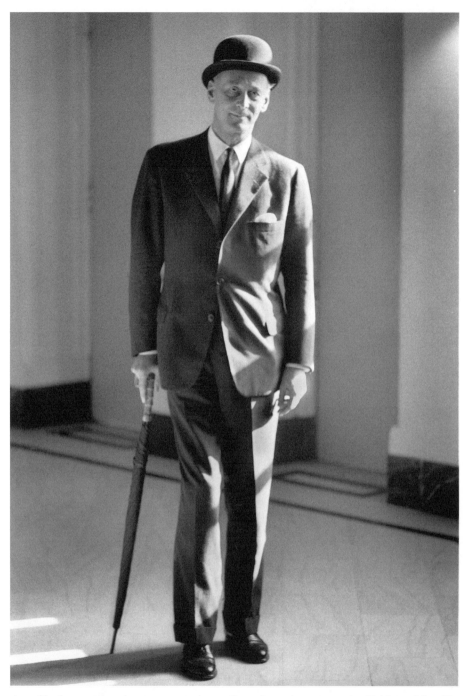

Arguably the most prominent opera manager of our time—in proper attire. Noblesse oblige. The title "Knight of the Opera" was unofficial, but he was a true Sir.... Now it's easy. See page 53 for the answer.

Name That Tune

In Tinseltown, the legend goes, movie plots are sketched out on the backs of envelopes in terms so simple even a movie-studio executive can understand them. Boy meets girl, boy loses girl, boy gets girl. What if the same were true of opera? (Boy meets girl, boy loses girl, everybody dies.) Herewith some famous opera plots, Spago-style.

1 Trés-studly war hero falls hard for nubile, dusky lass from wrong side of the river. The miscegenation theme could sell the opera all by itself, but wait, there's more: jealousy, hatred, and plenty of blood and guts. The ending's a knockout: buried alive in the pyramids! Can we get Mel and Julia?

2 Playboy putz hits on every broad he can get his hands on. The hook is, he's currently drilling the daughter of one of his cronies, a real clown. The fun begins when Dad gets wind of the affair and vows revenge. Ironic but downer ending could be changed if tests show the audiences prefer it upbeat. We see Bruce and Demi, with somebody like Danny DeVito as the jester.

3 Feminazis and Christian Coalitioners alike will love this highbrow babe-swap: two modern guys make a bet with a dirty old man from the neighborhood that within 24 hours each one will be able to bed the other fellow's gal. No way you say? Way! Think of it as *Bob & Carol & Ted & Alice* in period costume. A Merchant

and Ivory production starring Helena Bonham Carter and Jeremy Irons as the old rake.

4 You want something a little more ethnic? How about this: hot-blooded but dumb Basque soldier (don't ask me where the hell the Basques come from!) tumbles for mucho-fiery Gypsy cigarette girl. Bullfights, smugglers, sex—it's got it all! *Blood and Sand* updated, with Antonio Banderas in the Valentino part. The studio likes Eva Mendes for the gypsy girl.

5 Breakout possibilities with this bodice-ripper about a babelicious opera singer caught between her revolutionary lover and the sadistic Gestapo chief who's got the major-league hots for her. Forget the stuff about Napoleon in the script: we courageously set it in the Nazi period and let the chips fall where they may. Don't know about you, but we see Michael Caine as the bad guy with maybe Ethan Hawke or one of those pretty boys as the lover. Just the ticket for Scorsese if he's looking for work.

6 SFX abound in this fantasy-scifi epic (think George Lucas) about a superhero with feet of clay. Sure, the rough cut runs 17 hours or so but what the hell—so did Stroheim's *Greed* and we managed to cut that sucker down to size! Frank Aryan subject matter will appeal to Mr. and Mrs. Middle America, while the kids will go nuts over the giants, gods and dragons. And wait till you see what Industrial Light & Magic has cooked up in the way of flying horses!

| Beaucoup de latex means we probably can't get Gwyneth for female lead, plus we gotta do something about that name! Suggestions?

(continued from page 20)

As I was saying, what Mozart did was to transform opera into the most flexible dramatic structure yet devised. Think about it: plays—yes, even Shakespeare— exist largely on a single level; at their best, they combine poetry and drama into a seamless whole. Still, in the theater—or, as it is also known, the "legitimate stage" . . .

93 What's so "legitimate" about it?

Can I finish? The theater, fine as it is, still can only operate on a one-voice-at-a-time basis. An actor can deliver a monologue, or engage in a dialogue. Voices can overlap a little. But let three or more characters start to speak simultaneously and you've got chaos. The genius of opera is that two or more things can be happening all at once—and yet the listener has no trouble under- standing what is going on. Think not only of all the great trios, quartets and other small ensembles that dot the pages of operatic history, but of the massive choral numbers that ring out from Verdi and Wagner. Then imagine all those people shouting spoken dialogue at the same time.

94 Give an example from any Mozart opera.

In short, opera can be quite grand. But it can also follow the adage that less is more. As Mozart did in another great masterwork.

95 Name the character in a famous Mozart opera who absolutely dominates the action of every scene—and yet has very little solo music to sing, preferring instead to take on the color and sometimes even timbre of the other characters' voices.

96 Why is this?

97 Give the correct title of this opera. (Hint: it's not *Don Giovanni*.)

In sum, opera without Mozart is unthinkable. In just a few short decades of creative life, he perfected the art form, and pointed the way to the future.

Shavian Wit 'n' Wisdom

Before he became a great playwright, George Bernard Shaw was a great music critic—perhaps the greatest who ever lived. As a young journalist, he wrote first under the *nom de plume* of "Corno di Bassetto" (basset horn) and later under his own moniker. Shaw's musical gods were Mozart and Wagner, but he was extremely perceptive about a whole host of musical matters, bringing both his formidable intellect and his soon-to-be-famous Shavian wit to bear. Below, some vintage Shaw. Whom or what is he talking about?

1 In fitting the story of _____, MM Meilhac and Gille took for granted that their audience had read the novel upon which their libretto is founded. In France this assumption may have been justified, but the average Englishman is about as likely to have read the famous seventh volume of the *Mémoires et aventures d'un homme de qualité*, produced by the Prévost d'Exiles in 1731, as the average Frenchman is to have read *Clarissa*. Those who find the libretto bewildering will do well to read the novel, which is prodigiously superior to the opera.

2 Under these bettered circumstances, _____ revealed itself as a lighter and more fantastic work than it seemed before. Several passages, of which the shape and intention were obscured on the first occasion by timidity of execution, came out as burlesques of particular points in the reigning grand operas of 30 years ago, Meyerbeer being the chief victim of these pleasantries. Thus, the Barber's long cadenza on the name Morgiana, which sounded at the first performance like a somewhat overdone parody of the opera cadenza in general, became recognizable as a gibe at Peter's elaborate cadenza on the name Caterina in the tent scene in *L'Etoile du Nord*, from the last act of which opera, by the bye, _____ borrowed the leading phrase of Noureddin's first song.

3 It is not possible to give here any adequate account of _____'s claims to greatness as a composer. At present his music is hardly known in England except to those who study it in private. Public performances of it are few and far between, and, until Richter conducted the E-flat symphony here, nobody could have gathered from the vapid, hasty, trivial readings which were customary in our concert rooms that _____, judged by 19th-century standards, had any serious claim to his old-fashioned reputation.

4 The reader is now in a position to understand the tragedy of _____. He was a Mendelssohn Scholar. He was an organist (St. Somebody's, Chester Square). He wrote a symphony. He composed overtures, cantatas, oratorios. His masters were Goss and Sterndale Bennett himself. Of Magnificats he is guiltless; but two Te Deums and about a dozen anthems are among the fruits of his efforts to avoid the achievement of an effect. He has shown his reverence for the classics in the usual way by writing "additional accompaniments" to Handel's *Jeptha*; and now he has five columns in Grove and is a knight. What more could a serious musician desire? Alas! The same question might have been put to Tannhäuser at the singing bee in the Wartburg, before he broke out with his unholy longing for Venus.

5 This season a remarkable event sounded an alarm for stock companyism in opera. An Italian company came to London with one opera— _____—and astonished the frequenters of Covent Garden by the force and homogeneity of the impression made by its performance. The grip of the drama on the audience, the identification of the artists with their parts, the precision of execution, the perfect balance of the forces in action, produced an effect that, for the first time, justified the claims of Italian opera to rank as a form of serious drama united to purposeful music.

6 _____ is chiefly interesting as a proof that a really able literary man can turn out a much better opera than the average musician can, just as he can turn out a much more effective play than the average poet.

7 There is an old tradition that the _____ overture should be played against time so as to finish within three and a half minutes. There are 294 bars in the overture, and there are only 210 seconds in three and a half minutes. Consequently seven bars have to be played every five seconds.

8 Perfection is inextinguishable. If ever a nation tried hard to extinguish _____, one of the attainers of perfection, by the simple British method of ignoring him, that nation is Great Britain.

9 Last week the London press descanted on the fact that _____ stands with Bach and Beethoven as one of the greatest composers of all time. It also reported a naval court martial at which, among other matters, it transpired that a battleship, in a department needing eighteen men for its full equipment, put to sea with three.

What, it may be asked, is the connection between these two items? The connection is that they are both symptoms of a national weakness for writing and speaking without the smallest reference not only to facts, but to our own previous utterances on the same subjects.

10 I will now repeat my amusing performance of knocking Mr. Newman down flat with a single touch. He asks me, concerning a certain theme in _____, to look at it honestly and tell him whether it is not banality itself. Certainly it is. And now will Mr. Newman turn to the hackneyed little "half-close" out of which Handel made the "Hallelujah" chorus and tell me honestly whether it is not—and was not even in Handel's own time—ten times as banal?

Where Am I?

I am standing at the entrance to one of the world's great opera houses. It is a magnificent structure, designed by an important architect of its day and featuring frescoes by none other than Marc Chagall. Occupying a whole city block (or more), and strategically located at the confluence of several important streets and avenues, it dominates its setting like the royal thing of beauty that it is. "Rats" frolic on its rooftop as it soars over the city, one of the dominant civic buildings in a town full of them, and it also plunges several stories underground, to a dank, dark and mysterious sub-sub-sub basement wherein are buried hidden treasures and even darker legends. A grand staircase dominates the foyer, and although the auditorium itself is surprisingly small, rows upon rows of private boxes that soar to the painted ceiling ensure both the comfort and the discretion of its well-heeled patrons. The house was once home to the greatest spectacles of the age, and was practically synonymous with grace and grandeur. Now, it's most famous for its falling chandelier, its underground lake—and its ghost!

Well, I could be standing on the plaza at Lincoln Center in New York City. It too takes up more than a city block (in fact, it takes up several), stands at a crossroads and boasts murals by Chagall. Leave out the Chagall and I could be enjoying a *kaffee und kuchen* on the *Ringstrasse* in Vienna, surveying the magnificent Vienna State Opera House. But I'm not.

1 Where am I?

2 Whose ghost is it?

3 What's his problem?

4 Whose literary invention is he? (Or is he an invention at all?)

5 Whose musical invention is he?

6 What important musicological discovery was made there?

7 What important musicological discovery remains to be made there?

8 What connection does it have with the legend of the Opera Ghost?

I am standing in front of the Yellow Brick Brewery. It was built almost as much out of spite as out of love for the opera. Very quickly, though, it became even more snooty than the institution it was meant to snub (and, eventually, put out of business).

9 Where am I?

10 Why was the opera house built?

11 Who designed it?

12 Which other famous civic building in the same city is his design?

13 Name the street intersection where it was located.

14 What was the name, at the time, of the famous Square near which the opera house stood? What was it later called?

15 Where was the original, more favored site?

16 What year did the "brewery" open?

17 And with which opera?

18 Which, of course, was sung in what language?

19 Meanwhile, further downtown, a rival company was offering which opera?

20 Name the first opera house in the United States, and give its location.

21 What year did the "brewery" bite the dust?

22 Did anybody care?

23 Still, its destruction led to the saving of which other famous musical locale?

First the answers, then on to the 19th century!

Answers: Act One—The 18ᵗʰ Century: Mozart & Salieri

1 Jacopo Peri.

2 Florence, Italy.

3 1597.

4 *Dafne.*

5 Ottavio Rinuccini.

6 The wedding of Grand Duke Ferdinando I de'Medici and Christine of Lorraine. The bride wore white, Ilsa wore blue and the Germans wore gray.

7 Marco da Gagliano/*Dafne*; Claudio Monteverdi/*Orfeo, The Coronation of Poppea*; Henry Purcell/*Dido and Aeneas*; Marc-Antoine Charpentier/*L'Europe galante, Le Malade imaginaire*; George Frideric Handel/*Orlando, Rinaldo, Semele* and several million others; Johann Pepusch/*The Beggar's Opera*; Christoph Willibald Gluck/*Orfeo ed Euridice*; Franz Josef Haydn/*Il mondo della luna* and other now-forgotten works.

8 Johannes Chrysostomus Wolfgangus Theophilus Mozart.

9 No. "Amadé" was as close as he came.

10 It's the Latin version of "Theophilus."

11 Gottlieb.

12 "Love of God," or "Beloved of God."

13 Ask Peter Shaffer. Or maybe Salieri.

14 No.

15 Antonio Salieri, of course.

16 They were rivals, but not enemies.

17 That crazy old coot Salieri himself, for one, "confessed"' to murdering Mozart just before his own death in 1825.

18 Not a bit of it. He just wrote a heck of a play on the subject.

19 None other than Nikolai Rimsky-Korsakoff, in 1897.

20 Pushkin, whose "little drama" on the subject was written in 1830. Russian composers of the 19th century loved pirating Pushkin.

21 Only three: Mozart, Salieri and a blind violist who appears briefly to play—badly—part of an aria from *Don Giovanni*.

22 What do you think? The tenor, of course. Baritones are usually the bad guys.

23 Who knows? This little chamber opera is hardly ever performed. The score is written in a dry "Mozartian" style—anticipating what Rimsky's student, Stravinsky, would do in his neoclassical *The Rake's Progress* fifty years later.

24 If it didn't get revived in the wake of both the play and the movie of *Amadeus*, it probably never will be.

25 Here goes: *Les danaïdes*; *La grotta di Trofonio*; *Prima la musica e poi le parole*; *Tarare*; *Axur, rè d'Ormus*; *Falstaff, ossia Le tre burle*.

26 Mozart's work was *Der Schauspieldirektor*. The royal personage was Emperor Josef II.

27 Christian Ludwig Dieter (1757–1822). Must have been something in the water.

28 Lax copyright laws no doubt had something to do with it.

29 Not only that, it can make kids smarter too. In a book called *The Mozart Effect*, author Don Campbell, who has done considerable research on the subject, says that half an hour of listening to classical music equals roughly 10 mg of Valium. What's more, according to scientists at the University of California at Irvine, exposure to Mozart's music increases higher-brain activity. Students with musical experience also score higher on the SATs than those without—51 points higher in verbal, 39 points higher in math.

30 The first biography, which appeared in 1793, just two years after Mozart's death, was *Johannes Chrysostomus Wolfgang Gottlieb Mozart*, by Friederich Schlichtegroll. (Whew!) Next up was Franz Xaver Niemetschek, whose *Leben des k.k. Kapellmeisters Wolfgang Gottlieb Mozart nach Originalquellen beschrieben* hit the stands in 1808. Constanze Mozart, the composer's widow, hated the Schlichtegroll book so much she bought up and destroyed the entire second edition, and then cooperated with Niemetschek on a more flattering portrayal of her role in the great man's life. Finally, in 1828, the grieving widow published her late second husband George Nikolaus von Nissen's *Biographie W.A. Mozarts*. Constanze was one of the earliest examples of that now familiar archetype, the Professional Widow.

31 No. Mass graves were considered the right thing to do.

32 No. It was a little rainy—hardly bad weather for Vienna in December.

33 Because they make the death seem even more dramatic than it actually was. Hollywood has stolen this idea, shamelessly.

34 Beethoven, born in 1770, died in 1827. One of his biographers has the great man rising from his deathbed to shake a fist at the heavens just as a tremendous bolt of lightning strikes—and then he expires. Pure baloney.

35 Getting suckers to send him money.

36 Twenty—in other words, he was a middle-aged man.

37 *Le nozze di Figaro*, usually translated as *The Marriage of Figaro* but more accurately as Figaro's Wedding. The German gets it right: *Figaros Hochzeit*. The French original is the cause of all the confusion: *Le marriage de Figaro*.

38 This is one of those questions that you will have to answer for yourself. Keep reading the text.

39 *Le nozze di Figaro, Don Giovanni, Così fan tutte* and *Die Zauberflöte*.

40 Pierre Augustin Caron, 1732–99. He was the son of a Paris watchmaker who became watchmaker to the court of King Louis XV and a right royal favorite. He married the widow of a court official, tacking on the name de Beaumarchais and, with his new wealth, purchased the office of secretary to the King. During the American Revolution, he was also a gun-runner to the colonies.

41 The ridiculously prolific Rossini, who penned *The Barber of Seville* in 1816. I'd like to ask his mother what she was thinking when she hung that moniker on him. *Porco miserio*! as Toscanini used to say.

42 The play is *La mere coupable* (*The Guilty Mother*). Darius Milhaud set it to music in 1966, to no particular acclaim. More recently, John Corigliano used it as the springboard for *The Ghosts of Versailles*, which was premiered at the Metropolitan Opera in New York City in 1991.

43 If you know these operas by Milhaud—get a life!

L'Orestie
Les malheurs d'Orphée
Le pauvre matelot
Les Opéras-minutes
Christophe Columb

Corigliano's opera was his first.

44 They are either trying to have sex with someone, or are trying not to have sex with someone. It's that simple.

45 It is if the composer is doing it right.

46 Because love is a wonderful thing. It also makes the world go 'round. And it sure makes the stage a lot more interesting.

47 On the contrary: opera teaches children and other living things about how life should be lived. Or not, as the case may be.

48 Very few. And they're hardly ever performed. Even something like Puccini's *Suor Angelica*, which purports to be about a cloistered nun, is really about sex.

49 His name was Lorenzo da Ponte, and yes, he was.

50 Dirty young man perhaps. While "researching" his libretto for *Don Giovanni* he not only consulted with the legendary lover Casanova, but—oh, let him tell it: "A beautiful young girl of sixteen was living in my house with her mother. (I should have wished to love her as a daughter, but …) She came to my room whenever I rang the bell, which was fairly often, and particularly when my inspiration seemed to begin to cool . . ."

51 In New York City, where he became the first professor of romance languages at Columbia University and a saucy memoirist. He's buried in Manhattan.

52 Rafaello.

53 Marcellina (who's been trying to get Figaro to marry her for defaulting on an old debt) and Dr. Bartolo, Figaro's arch-enemy, who doesn't recognize his son until late in the game. After which, of course, all is forgiven.

54 Susanna.

55 The Countess.

56 Susanna.

57 The Count.

58 Cherubino.

59 Anna Maria Pertl.

60 Maria Anna Walburga Ignatia.

61 Maria Anna Thekla—the "Bäsle."

62 Don't ask me.

63 Leopold and Anna Maria had seven children, five of whom died in infancy. Wolfgang and his sister Nannerl, four years older, were the only survivors.

64 Did he ever! Here's an example from Solomon: in his letter of 10 May 1780, he spins a rapid series of sexual puns, enjoining his cousin to "blow into my behind. It's splendid food, may it do you good"; he refers to her "fascinating beauty (*visibilia* and *invisibilia*)"; describes himself as "very soft, and I like mustard too, particularly with beef"; and writes that "one has the purse and another has the gold," the interesting idea being, of course, to put the one into the other.

65 How about the "Kiss My Arse" canon?

66 Because a man's personal life has little or nothing to do with his professional life. Or a woman's for that matter. In other words, in art, character doesn't count. Just ask Wagner, about whom there's more in the next chapter.

67 They were if they were doing it right.

68 The Freemasons.

69 The Abbé Jean Terrasson (1670–1750), a French priest, principally his 1731 fiction *Sethos, a History or Biography*, based on *Unpublished Memoirs of Ancient Egypt*. Terrasson's Europeanized, quasi-Christianized notion of ancient Egypt, written before the discovery of the Rosetta Stone in 1799, was about as authentic as Japanese notions of Westerners before Commodore Perry showed up. Like Marx, it was hooey. But, like Marxism, it was extremely influential on generations of forward-thinking intellectuals in Europe for several generations. Go figure.

70 Ignaz von Born, the leader of the Masonic Lodge of Crowned Hope in Vienna, who wrote a treatise called "About the Mysteries of Egypt" for a new Masonic journal. Von Born sought to prove that the ancient Egyptians were the forerunners of Western culture, and that their ethos survived in the customs of the Masons.

71 Two: *Thamos, King of Egypt* and *The Magic Flute.*

72 Emanuel Schikaneder.

73 He is sometimes depicted as Egyptian, sometimes as Japanese.

74 Papagena is, as she informs us, "18 years and two minutes" old. Papageno is ten years older.

75 Depends on whose side you're on, or which act you're watching. In Act 1, the Queen of the Night has her minions, the Three Ladies, rescue Tamino from the clutches of a serpent (killing snakes played a large role in Masonic theory), and warns the prince about the evil Sarastro who has kidnapped her daughter. In the second act, however, we are told that the exact opposite is true—that the Queen is evil, Sarastro good and that the "kidnapping" is really a kind of rescue/deprogramming operation.

76 Not much. For if Sarastro is good, then what is he doing with a servant like Monostatos, who eventually betrays him by allying himself with the Queen of the Night (and is destroyed by Sarastro at the opera's conclusion)? And if the Queen is so bad, why does she rescue Tamino and set him on his quest for her beloved daughter, Pamina? John Le Carré could probably make something out of this obvious disinformation/double-cross plot, but

Schikaneder couldn't and didn't. Luckily for us, Mozart did.

77 This gets us to the very heart of the discussion of opera, and Mozart's contribution to it.

78 I don't know. My eight-year-old daughter asked me this ten years ago. But based on recent research, each of us meets approximately 50,000 people in the course of a lifetime. So let's put Mozart at 30,000, on the high side.

79 OK, here we go:

17th century: Stefano Landi, Luigi Rossi, Pier Francesco Cavalli, Marc'Antonio Cesti, Alessandro — not Domenico! — Scarlatti (all from Italy).

18th century: Jean Baptiste Lully, Jean-Philippe Rameau (France); Karl Ditters von Dittersdorf (Germany); Domenico Cimarosa (Italy).

80 I told you so.

81 Does the name Henry Purcell mean anything to you? Not to mention the aforementioned Handel and Haydn.

82 Because we're here to learn about the meaning of opera—not to play a trivia game.

83 Why, none other than that famous man of letters, Dr. Samuel Johnson, displaying his famous acerbic wit.

84 I don't. But Boswell probably did.

85 He did. But he was also intimately involved in the intellectual life of London—you might say he *was* the intellectual life of London at the time—and so got caught up in the Great Handel Wars.

86 Which were about the struggles between two major English opera companies—who performed, of course, in Italian. From 1710 to 1740, the German-import Handel dominated the London operatic scene. Handel raised the baroque opera—best known to us as *opera seria*—to its highest form. It may strike you as a dramaturgically indecipherable sequence of interchangeable arias, each of which repeats itself more often than your senile old uncle (the so-called *da capo* aria), but to connoisseurs of the genre it's just swell.

87 Handel was a great composer, but he appeared to have had great difficulty in running his opera company. Then, as now, opera was extremely expensive, and opera companies like Handel's needed serious funding in order for them to make a go of it.

88 At his best, he could write an opera a year.

89 They did indeed.

90 Castrati, whose meaning is self-evident.

91 Fella named Senesino.

92 There were indeed. By name: Francesca Cuzzoni and Faustina Bordoni. The rivalry nearly destroyed Cuzzoni's career. Sopranos haven't changed much since then.

93 I don't know. "Legitimate" used to refer to the distinction between "serious" theater and the many different varieties of musical entertainment that were also available earlier in the century. Today, however, that distinction is pretty much down to Neil Simon and Andrew Lloyd Webber.

94 How about the great sextet in Act 3 of *Figaro*? Here, in a welter of revelation and discovery, the plot of the opera suddenly is turned on its head.

95 *Don Giovanni*, of course.

96 We're not quite sure. It may have been that Mozart was making an implicit dramatic statement. Or that his original leading man, Luigi Bassi (who was only 21 at the premiere in Prague), wasn't up to any greater vocal challenge. But it doesn't matter: as with *Figaro*, in which Mozart transfigured the conventions of opera buffa by humanizing each and every one of the main characters, in *Don Giovanni*, Mozart wrote the world's first (and perhaps only) fully successful blend of stark drama and high comedy—the "dramma giocoso" of one's dreams.

97 *Il dissoluto punito, o sia Il Don Giovanni*

Answers: Books into Operas

1 *Der Templar und die Jüdin*, by Heinrich Marschner; *Ivanhoe*, by Sir Arthur Sullivan.

2 *Roméo et Juliette*, by Gounod; *I Capuleti e I Montecchi*, by Bellini.

3 *Billy Budd*, by Britten.

4 *Lily*, by Leon Kirchner.

5 *Lulu*, by Berg.

6 *War and Peace*, by Prokofiev.

7 *Tom Jones*, by Stephen Oliver.

8 *The Scarlet Letter*, by Walter Damrosch.

9 *La donna del lago*, by Rossini.

10 *Wuthering Heights*, by Bernard Herrmann; *Wuthering Heights*, by Carlisle Floyd.

11 *Werther*, by Massenet.

12 *Der Corregidor*, by Hugo Wolf.

13 *Lear*, by Aribert Reimann.

14 *Regina*, by Marc Blitzstein.

15 *Die lustigen Weiber von Windsor*, by Otto Nicolai; *Falstaff*, by Verdi; and *Sir John in Love*, by Ralph Vaughan Williams.

16 *The Turn of the Screw*, by Britten.

17 *Curlew River*, by Britten.

18 *The Fall of the House of Usher*, by Philip Glass.

19 *From the House of the Dead*, by Leoš Janáček.

20 *Paradise Lost*, by Krzystof Penderecki.

Answers: Politically Incorrect

1 Wowkle, in Puccini's *La Fanciulla del West.*

2 Monostatos, in Mozart's *The Magic Flute.*

3 Sportin' Life, in *Porgy and Bess.*

4 Don Alvaro, in *La forza del destino.*

5 *La Bohème.*

6 *Aida.*

7 *Hänsel und Gretel.*

8 Don José, in *Carmen.*

9 Countess Geschwitz in Berg's *Lulu.*

10 *Rigoletto.*

Answers: Name That Tune

1 Verdi's *Aida.*

2 Verdi's *Rigoletto.*

3 Mozart's *Così fan tutte.*

4 Bizet's *Carmen.*

5 Puccini's *Tosca.*

6 Wagner's *Der Ring des Nibelungen*, Brünnhilde.

Answers: Shavian Wit 'n' Wisdom

1 *Manon*, by Massenet.

2 *The Barber of Bagdad*; Peter Cornelius.

3 Mozart.

4 Sir Arthur Sullivan.

5 Verdi's *Otello*.

6 Boito's *Mefistofele*.

7 *The Marriage of Figaro*.

8 Gluck.

9 Richard Wagner.

10 Strauss's *Elektra*, over which Shaw and Wagner's biographer Ernest Newman battled furiously.

Answers: Where Am I?

1 At the Place de l'Opera, in front of the Paris Opera House, designed by Charles Garnier.

2 Erik, the Phantom of the Opera.

3 A hideously deformed composer, he seeks the perfect soprano for the lead role in his new opera.

4 Gaston Leroux, the French Journalist who wrote *The Phantom of the Opera*. The detailed and accurate description of the Paris Opera was based on Leroux's firsthand experience with the house, including the legend of a ghost that haunted the rafters.

5 Andrew Lloyd Webber, who made the Phantom the hero of his hit musical. Also Ken Hill, who had the idea even before Webber.

6 The music critic Andrew Porter discovered the original version of Verdi's opera *Don Carlos*, which was written for the Paris Opera and received its first performance there in 1867.

7 Hidden away in a sub-basement, and sealed for a century, there is a time capsule that is marked simply "Gift of M. Alfred Clark." Clark was the director of the Berliner Record Company in Paris in 1907, and the room is thought to contain gramophone records of the period.

8 The room in which the gramophone records are buried, near which the skeleton of Erik the Phantom is found at the end of the novel, really exists.

9 The old Metropolitan Opera House in New York City.

10 Because some of the nouveau riche, such as the Astors, had been snubbed in their attempt to get fancy boxes at the Academy of Music on 14th Street. So they went and built their own.

11 The principal architect was Josiah Cleaveland Cady, best known as a church and hospital architect; the old Met was his first and last theater.

12 The American Museum of Natural History.

13 Broadway, between 39th and 40th Streets.

14 Longacre Square, soon thereafter to be renamed Times Square.

15 Across the street from Grand Central Station.

16 1883.

17 Gounod's *Faust*, which reigned for many years as the most oft-performed piece in the Met's repertory.

18 Italian. When the Met advertised an "Italian season" in those days, it wasn't kidding. Gounod, Wagner, Rimsky—it didn't matter.

19 The Academy of Music was featuring Bellini's *La sonnambula*.

20 The Théâtre du Spectacle in New Orleans.

21 1966, just after a farewell gala conducted by Leopold Stokowski. Then came the wrecker's ball, much to the relief of Met manager and curmudgeon-in-chief Rudolf Bing, who couldn't wait to get out of there for the far better facilities of the new Met.

22 Did they ever. There was a huge "Save the Met" movement, to no avail. Truth to tell, as far as opera professionals were concerned, the antiquated and cramped building wasn't worth saving.

23 Carnegie Hall.

Answers: Act One Photo Captions

1 Pages 7, 21–22: Sir Rudolf Bing, General Manager of the Metropolitan Opera in New York 1950–1972.

2 Page 14–15: *La Bohème* by Giacomo Puccini.

3 Page 19: Luciano Pavarotti.

Opposite: George London in *Die Walküre*

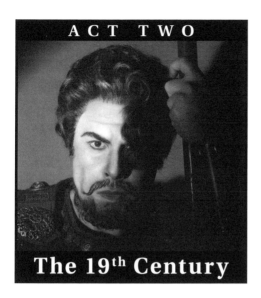

ACT TWO

The 19th Century

Beethoven, Wagner, Tchaikovsky & Verdi

T he 19th century is, for most opera fans, the highest flowering of the operatic art. Most of the works in the so-called "standard repertory" come out of it, as well as many of the singers we consider "legendary" today. The 19th century, which includes everything from Schubert and Beethoven to Mahler and Brahms, is roughly synonymous with the Romantic movement in music—and that is the kind of music most folks love best. Like it or lump it.

Let's get into the 19th century with a few questions based on the paragraph above. Look out, they're tricky!

1 How many operas did Schubert write?

2 Name 'em! (Some of 'em, anyway.)

3 How many of them were hits?

4 How many operas did Beethoven write?

5 Name the subtitle of Beethoven's last opera.

6 What does all Beethoven's trouble with this opera prove?

7 How many operas did Mahler write?

8 Really?

Not all great 19th-century composers tried their hands at opera. Not even some of the most famous songwriters in classical-music history.

9 Name some who didn't.

10 Surely you jest. Or at least fib a little.

In fact, it seems that the more accomplished the song-writer, the less likely he was to have written a great opera—or any opera at all.

11 Name other great lieder composers who flopped at opera, or didn't even try it.

12 Name one great lieder writer who was also a great opera composer.

13 How do you explain this?

14 You keep using that word, lieder. What's this lieder stuff, anyway?

15 Well, what's the difference between writing a song and writing an opera?

Luckily for us, there were plenty of great composers who found their *métier* in opera, taking the form bequeathed to them by Mozart and turning it into the most flexible mode of dramatic expression the world has ever seen.

In the early 19th century, the operatic action was to be found (as it was earlier) in France, Germany and Italy. Quickly, though, Paris became the center of serious operatic activity, and composers from all over Europe flocked to the City of Light.

16 Name three great foreign-born composers active in Paris in the early 19th century and at least one major work associated with each of them.

17 Didn't one of them have a big (if negative) influence on a very, very, very famous composer?

18 What happened to all the French composers?

19 And did Beethoven go to Paris as well?

20 So did Paris go to Beethoven?

We don't ordinarily think of Beethoven as an opera composer. By and large, Beethoven's vocal music is what singers call "ungrateful" . . .

21 What does that mean?

22 I thought "ungrateful" was what Beethoven's nasty nephew Karl was all about. Give me an example of this so-called vocal ungratefulness.

23 What—did he get lucky?

But in *Fidelio* Beethoven created one of the operatic repertory's enduring masterpieces. It's the best place to begin our discussion of Romantic opera.

24 Beethoven was a notorious prude who thought Mozart's *Don Giovanni* an immoral opera. And yet in *Fidelio* he wrote an opera whose main character is a transvestite. How do you explain that?

25 In the opera, what are the sexual consequences of this cross-dressing?

26 Where in the world did he get this notion?

27 Not counting *The Rocky Horror Show*, name some other well-known operas that feature cross-dressing.

The role of Leonore is one of the toughest in all of opera. Only the greatest or most foolhardy of dramatic sopranos undertakes this monster of a part. And only the greatest of tenors can handle the demands of Florestan. And while we're on the subject, it takes a pretty darn good conductor to pull the whole thing off. This is, after all, Beethoven.

28 Why?

29 How come the musical style of *Fidelio* changes so radically from beginning to end? Didn't Beethoven know what he was doing?

30 Name another opera whose heroine is named Leonore.

31 What is the name of Leonore's big aria?

32 What is the name of Florestan's dungeon aria?

33 What's Florestan doing in the jug anyway?

34 Name another great opera about a political prisoner. (Hint: think 20th century.)

35 Is Rocco really a bad guy?

36 Well, then, who is the villain? What happens to him in the end?

37 Why does the orchestra play the *Leonore* Overture No. 3 between the two scenes of the second act?

38 Isn't there a Mozart opera that 19th-century conductors monkeyed with as well?

39 Does Marzelline ever find true love, and if so with whom?

For all its flaws, *Fidelio* stands as *the* great opera of the early 19th century. Its only conceivable rival is another opera written little more than a decade later, a work that had a tremendous influence on the course of Romantic opera.

40 Name this spooky piece, performed relatively rarely outside its home country, that fired the imagination of one of the 19th century's greatest composers.

41 Whose imagination did it set aflame?

42 Name another composer from the same country whose works form an important transition between the two men we're discussing.

43 What are the best bits?

44 If it's so all-fired good, why ain't it famous?

45 Did this composer write anything else we might have heard of? Or is worth finding out about?

About the same time, there arose in Italy a school of operatic writing that was to determine the course of Italian opera—at least melodically—for the next century or so.

46 What is it called—and why?

47 Name the great composers of this particular style.

48 Name a half-dozen or so of the most famous exemplars.

49 Doesn't one of these operas have a trumpet lick that sounds suspiciously like the main theme from *The Godfather*?

50 Aren't there laws against stuff like that?

51 Of the not-so-famous exemplars, name as many as you can think of.

52 How should I feel about bel canto opera? I mean, is it intellectually respectable?

Of course, not all great operas of the 19th century were German or Italian. The French were still in there pitching, and none more effectively than . . . well, who?

53 Name the Louisiana-born composer whose contributions to one of the most popular operas ever written makes him, by far, the most-performed American composer of all time.

54 Name some of his other operas.

55 One of his ballets, believe it or not, has a title that connects it to the murder of Nicole Brown Simpson. Which is it?

56 What other famous opera did he work on?

57 Which famous Frenchman completed this composer's last opera?

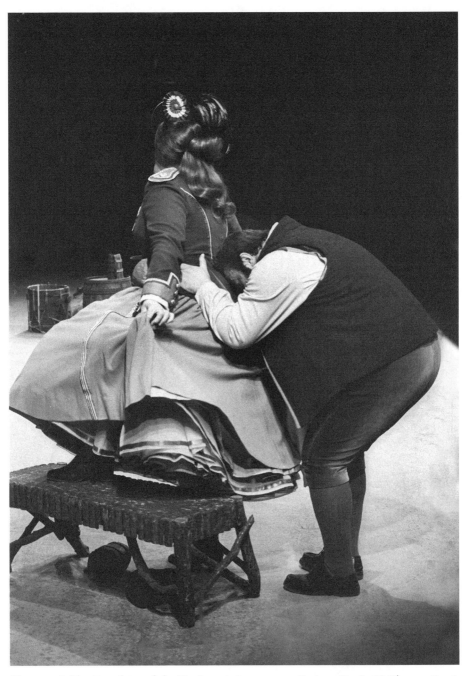

The opera is The Daughter of the Regiment, *its composer Gaetano Donizetti. The question is who are the two stars of this Metropolitan Opera performance playing hide-and-seek? The answer is revealed on page 86.*

Another country full of operatic fun was Mother Russia, where a group of composers who called themselves "The Mighty Five" or "The Mighty Handful" (and what a handful they were!) were busy forging the soul of a new kind of *echt*-Russian opera. Frankly nationalistic, they were determined to cast off western European influences in favor of an authentically Russian sound, and to that end they employed folk songs and other "Russian" devices to distinguish their music from the French or the Germans.

58 Name "The Mighty Five."

59 Name some of their works.

60 What's *William Ratcliff*'s claim to fame, and what's odd about it?

61 Who, in their estimation, was their spiritual father (musically speaking)?

62 What did he write?

(continued on page 66)

More Name That Tune

1 We've set this one in old Mother Russia: swaggering swordsman Gene (can we get Mel?) cruelly breaks the heart of impressionable young virgin Tanya (Winona Ryder) amid the snowy landscapes and glittering Imperial balls. Just the thing for David Lean if he weren't dead. Calling Anthony Minghella!

2 He loves her and she loves him but unfortunately she marries a German guy named Al instead, leading to all kinds of psychological damage. We like Gary Oldman in his faux-Dracula mode for the title role and a foreign honey like Emmanuelle Beart for the girl. Think of this one as high-class *Fatal Attraction* in reverse; if the suicide ending doesn't test well with Middle America, we'll get a rewrite.

3 Great minds think alike: across town we hear they're developing another he-loves-her-and-she-loves-him-but-unfortunately-she's-already-married-to-some-schmuck scenario, this one set in southern Italy. Maybe we ought to think about acquiring it: the weather in Germany stinks and the food—forget about it! Olive-oil weeper with Cher and Nicholas Cage in the leads. Coppola directs, of course.

4 The Love That Dare Not Speak Its Name—is now shouting it! So let's hop on the gay bandwagon before it rolls away with this tale of an aging pretty-boy (he's a writer in Tommy Mann's original script, but we can change him to something more sympathetic. How about an aging movie director?) who goes on vacation to the seashore only to fall in love with a young boy. He eventually dies of cholera, but we can change it to AIDS to be more topical. It may be a stretch, but we see a coupla somebodies like Sly Stallone (did you say Oscar!?) and Leonardo di Caprio above the line. What do you think?

5 Not since the heyday of Vic Mature and Debra Paget has there been a costume epic like this one: Nero's the king, and what the king wants, oh baby, the king gets! And he wants the oh-so-oo-la-la Poppy (Alicia Silverstone or Drew Barrymore, it says here), whom he's eyeballing as a Replacement Wife for his current ball-and-chain. Bed-hopping abounds with a little transvestitism and suicide thrown in for the kids. Joel Schumacher's a natural to direct, and if we can't get Russell Crowe to play Nero, well then it's not worth doing.

6 Everybody loves Paris, especially young lovers. We set this one on the Left Bank, where struggling artists dream of glory while trying to stay warm. She (Julia Stiles) is a seamstress with TB (but who knew?). He (Matt Dillon) is a poet or something. Warm and fuzzy comedy turns tragic with her death (think *Love Story*), but writers have already come up with a happy ending in Hawaii in case we need it.

They Won't Sing—Don't Ask Them

A surprising number of operas feature important roles in which a major character never opens his or her mouth in song. Shhhh. . . . Match the non-singing one to the opera.

1 Count Heinrich.

2 Bassa Selim.

3 Sir Edgar.

4 Fra Redemptor.

5 John Bagtry and Belle.

(continued from page 63)

Meanwhile, over in a corner pretty much all by himself stood the figure of Tchaikovsky, who turned out to be the greatest of them all. Tchaikovsky wrote operas throughout his career, and while not all of them are gems, at least two are in the repertoires of every major opera company.

63 Which two?

64 On the works of which Russian poet are their librettos based?

65 Who wrote the librettos?

66 Name the third Tchaikovsky opera based on Pushkin.

67 Name at least five other Tchaikovsky operas.

68 One of Tchaikovsky's operas shares its name with a work by Liszt. Which one?

69 Another Tchaikovsky opera shares its name with a work by Gilbert and Sullivan. Which one?

70 Still another Tchaikovsky opera shares its title with two other operas. Name the composers.

71 Speaking of Sir Arthur Sullivan, he wrote a "grand" opera in addition to his work with W.S. Gilbert. Its name, please.

Tchaikovsky, it is true, partook rather more enthusiastically of western European musical developments than "The Mighty Handful." But Tchaikovsky poured plenty of Russian spirit—not to mention scenes from his own tortured life—into his operas.

72 Which early Tchaikovsky opera has at least four recognizable Russian folk songs in its score?

73 Which early Tchaikovsky opera was, musically speaking, a reworking of his first opera, *The Voyevoda*, especially in its first act?

74 In May of 1877, Tchaikovsky received his fateful love letter from Antonina Milyukova and shortly thereafter began to compose a new operatic scene in which a young woman writes a passionate love letter to an older man. Who says life doesn't imitate art? Name the opera.

75 True or false: Tchaikovsky committed suicide.

Tchaikovsky and the others were certainly great opera composers. But the man whose very name has come to symbolize the vibrant form of opera we know and love best is . . . Yes, friends, I'm referring to none other than Mean Joe Green—whoops! I mean Giuseppe Verdi. *Mamma mia*! Now that's Italian opera!

Wherever Verdi fans gather, you'll get arguments about which of his 28 operas (29, if you count the two versions of *Simon Boccanegra*) is the greatest.

76 OK, smart guy—which one is it?

Well, some folks will hold out for middle-period Verdi, the time of such popular operas as *Rigoletto*, *Il Trovatore* and *La Traviata*. It's this kind of opera that generally comes to mind when we think of Verdi (it came to mind when Irving Thalberg and the Marx Brothers thought of Verdi, too) . . .

77 Speaking of whom, which opera gets the full Groucho in *A Night at the Opera*?

78 Which famous playwright coauthored the madcap screenplay?

79 What was the name of Groucho's character, and whose life did he make miserable?

. . . but if you ask me (which is, after all, what you're doing by reading this book), the real genius of Verdi is most fully expressed in the later works. And particularly by two operas: *Don Carlos* and *Otello*.

80 On whose great play did Verdi base *Don Carlos*?

81 Name two other plays by the same dramatist set by Verdi.

82 In Beethoven's "political prisoner" opera referred to above, what is the connection to Verdi's *Don Carlos*?

83 Sometimes we see the title given as *Don Carlo*. What gives?

84 So what language should it be sung in?

85 What's so great about *Don Carlos*?

86 Is there anything about it that isn't first-rate?

87 What's all this about the title character being an infant?

88 When Princess Eboli sings her aria, "O don fatale," is she singing about Don Carlos or not?

89 Does Elisabeth love Don Carlos, Philip, both or neither?

90 What the heck happens at the end of this opera? I mean, is that really the ghost of Charles V, or an old monk, or is Carlos hallucinating or what?

(continued on page 72)

No—this is not a scene from Godfather IV. *Photographer Henry Grossman caught this group of innocent card players in a San Francisco hotel room many moons ago, killing . . . time only. You will have no problem identifying the bearded "gambler"— it's Luciano Pavarotti. But how about his friends? All of them, but one, very successful colleagues. The lady standing is the mother of . . . ? Get another look on pages 82–83.*

(continued from page 69)

Like *Don Carlos*, *Otello* is based on a famous play. I won't insult your intelligence by asking you to name the playwright . . .

91 Go ahead, try me. I dare you!

. . . but I will ask you to name not only the playwright, but a bunch of other things pertaining to *Otello* as well. So how about . . .

92 The name of the librettist.

93 The name of the semi-famous opera he composed himself.

94 The name of the very famous opera for which he wrote the libretto under a pseudonym.

95 The dumb thing he wrote that almost sank his collaboration with Verdi before it had even begun.

96 The name of the other Shakespeare opera he wrote with Verdi.

97 The third Shakespeare play that occupied Verdi for years, and which he never managed to turn into an opera.

98 Why the name of the opera is spelled differently from that of the play.

99 Until about a year before the premiere, what was the opera's working title?

100 The name of the cellist in the orchestra the night of *Otello*'s premiere who went on to a spectacular career as a conductor.

101 Name another famous composer who wrote an opera called *Otello*.

Don't get me wrong. It's not as if I don't like *Aida* or even the darkly tragic *Simon Boccanegra* (in its revised 1881 version), the two operas that came between *Don Carlos* and *Otello*. I enjoy seeing a tenor entombed in the Pyramids as much as the next guy. And everybody likes live elephants on the stage, except maybe the fellow who has to clean up after them. I even enjoy Verdi's last opera, *Falstaff*, despite the fact that it contains only one melody, and its high point of hilarity is reached when Plump Jack gets chucked in the river along with the rest of the dirty laundry.

But *Otello* is such a singularly magnificent achievement that, for me, it stands unrivaled as Verdi's most perfect work. In many respects it's better than the original.

102 Wait just a minute! Are you saying that Verdi and Boito successfully rewrote the sainted Will Shakespeare?

That's exactly what I'm saying—in this instance. Boito's tight, practically cinematic libretto strips the story down to its pure essence as a tragic love story, and Verdi's music supplies a dramatic dimension of which Shakespeare never dreamed. I'm sorry, but that's just the way it is. So stop bugging me and let's get on to the questions.

103 The act of Shakespeare's play that Boito eliminated.

104 The translation of Shakespeare from which he worked.

105 The difference in pronunciation in the name of the heroine between play and opera.

106 The great set piece that Boito made up out of whole cloth.

107 The apposite musico-dramatic device that Verdi used to delineate the difference between Otello and Desdemona on one hand, and Iago on the other.

From the middle of the 19th century on, the two greatest musical dramatists were, by common consent, Verdi and Richard Wagner.

108 Which Verdi opera was accused of being "too Wagnerian"?

They could not have been more different. Where Verdi saw himself and his great works, quite rightly, as the culmination of the Italian operatic tradition, Wagner was an iconoclast who declared himself the sun around which the world of opera would henceforth revolve. And, wouldn't you know it, he was pretty much right.

Before we leave Verdi, though, a couple of last questions about the man himself:

109 What was Verdi's second wife's name?

110 What was the name of the charity home Verdi founded for old musicians in Milan?

111 Which Verdi opera is set in Boston, and why?

112 Is it possible to translate the title of *La Traviata*, and if so how do you do it?

113 What does "Viva Verdi!" mean?

114 Which aristocratic title did Verdi decline?

(continued on page 80)

Who Said It?

The well-chosen *bon mot* or amusing aperçu has long been an integral part of the opera experience. Match the quips below with the wits who articulated them.

1 The actor apes a man—at least in shape
The opera performer apes an ape.
a) Groucho Marx
b) Ambrose Bierce
c) Sir John Betjeman

2 If an opera cannot be played by an organ-grinder—as Puccini and Verdi's melodies were played—then that opera is not going to achieve immortality.
a) George Raft
b) James Levine
c) Sir Thomas Beecham

3 Opera in English is, in the main, just about as sensible as baseball in Italian.
a) H.L. Mencken
b) Damon Runyon
c) Ed Sullivan

4 Nobody really sings in opera. They just make loud noises.
a) Luciano Pavarotti
b) Joan Sutherland
c) Amelita Galli-Curci

5 Of all the affected, sapless, soulless, beginningless, endless, topless, bottomless, topsyturviest, scrannel-pipiest, tongs and boniest doggerel of sounds I ever endured the deadliest of, that eternity of nothing was the deadliest.
a) John Ruskin
b) Harry S. Truman
c) Harold C. Schonberg

6 We went to Mannheim and attended a shivaree—otherwise an opera—the lone called *Lohengrin*. The banging and slamming and booming and crashing were something beyond belief.
a) Mark Twain
b) Sam Clemens
c) A Tramp Abroad

7 If you will only take the precaution to go in long enough after it commences and to come out long before it is over, you will not find it wearisome.
a) Queen Victoria
b) Oscar Wilde
c) George Bernard Shaw

8 Music is a woman. She must be loved by the poet, must surrender herself to him, in order

that the new art-work of the future may be born . . .
a) Casanova
b) Don Juan
c) Richard Wagner

9 I have occasionally remarked that the only entirely creditable incident in English history is the sending of £100 to Beethoven on his deathbed by the London Philharmonic Society; and it is the only one that historians never mention.
a) Eamon de Valera
b) George Bernard Shaw
c) John Lennon

10 Is Wagner actually a man? Is he not rather a disease? Everything he touches falls ill: he has made music sick.
a) Friedrich Nietzsche
b) Mark Twain
c) Adolf Hitler

11 I like Wagner's music better than anybody's. It is so loud that one can talk the whole time without people hearing what one says.
a) Oscar Wilde
b) Mark Twain
c) Nietzsche

12 If unmelodious was the song, it was a hearty note and strong.
a) *The New York Times*
b) Sir Walter Scott
c) Muhammed Ali

Nobody will question that Richard Tucker was the most popular operatic tenor "born in the USA." Canio in Leoncavallo's Pagliacci (this page) was one of his favorite roles. The photos on the opposite page document two last-minute rituals before a performance: check makeup and stick a penny in the shoe. The "good luck" coin is deposited by Tucker's wife, Sarah. Here is the question: Sarah's sister was the spouse of another famous American tenor. Can you name him? See page 111.

(continued from page 75)

And so we come to Verdi's great contemporary and rival, Richard Wagner. Let's begin with some basic Wagner lore.

115 Who was Wagner's dad? Was it Mr. Wagner?

116 In the 19th century, who was Wagner's biggest fan?

117 In the 20th century who was Wagner's biggest fan?

118 Didn't this avid fan have a somewhat similar problem, family-wise, as Wagner?

I dwell on Wagner's extra-musical ramifications because they're important. It's impossible to understand the history of the 20th century without some understanding of Wagner, and so if we talk as much about Wagner's life and times as we do about his music, there's a very good reason for it.

Let's start with some easy ones:

119 If you could compare Wagner to one 18th-century composer in particular (philosophically speaking), who would it be and why?

120 Besides himself, who was Wagner's favorite composer?

121 Name the three early Wagner operas that nobody performs today.

122 What is the subtitle of that third failed opera?

123 Which opera, sometimes performed today but best known for its stirring overture, came next?

124 Which Wagner opera was inspired by a terrifying sea voyage?

125 Which Wagner opera features the goddess Venus in a starring role?

126 Which opera contains the Wedding March, beloved of every bride and groom?

127 Just what the heck is the Ring of the Nibelung, anyway, and why is everybody so desirous of it?

128 Which is the first of the *Ring* operas?

129 Did Wotan overpay for Valhalla?

130 Is the rhythm of the "Ride of the Valkyries" best expressed as "I'm SICK on a see-saw" or "I'm sick on a SEE-saw"?

131 In which opera does The Wanderer appear, and why does he wear a broad-brimmed hat?

132 What's Waltraute's problem?

133 Who gets the last words in the *Ring* and what are they?

(continued on page 84)

If you still have difficulties recognizing the three card players, check their first names on the score card. "Lucky" is NOT one of them. If all else fails, see page 111.

(continued from page 81)

134 Where does Tristan come from? Isolde? King Marke?

135 The opening phrase of *Tristan und Isolde* is one of the most important in the history of music, and many later composers have acknowledged their debt to it by explicit quotation. Who was the first to quote it, and in which opera?

136 Who wrote the opera *Hans Sachs*?

137 Where does the action of Wagner's last opera take place?

138 At the end of his life, who else was Wagner considering as a subject for an opera?

If you've answered all of the above correctly, congratulations—you've just named all of Wagner's operas, in order! Some more Wagneriana:

139 True or false: Wagner considered moving to America.

140 Speaking of Philadelphia, which minor piece did Wagner compose for the Centennial Exposition in 1876?

141 The year 1876 saw a rather more important event in Wagner's life. What was it?

142 What is the name of the small town in Bavaria where Wagner built his theater?

143 What does the name of Wagner's house, the Villa Wahnfried, mean?

144 Where is Wagner buried?

145 What was the name of Wagner's arch-enemy, and in which opera was he parodied?

146 What's the full title of *Tannhäuser*?

147 Why?

148 I hear these funny whispers from time to time about Wagner and Mad King Ludwig. What was the nature of their relationship?

149 True or false: Wagner wore silk underwear.

150 True or false: Wagner was a virulent, practicing anti-Semite.

151 How many children did Wagner have with his first wife?

152 What famous composer's daughter became Wagner's second wife?

153 What was unusual about the birth of Wagner's daughter, Isolde?

154 Weren't there any hard feelings?

I guess the point about Wagner is that you can be an anti-Semitic, greedy, obnoxious, self-centered philanderer and still be a great composer. Which means there's hope for all of us. We'll need it.

Not that you did not know the answer already. . . . The regiment's daughter is a dame. Joan Sutherland. She inspires young Tonio to a treacherous vocal tour de force, the aria "Ah, mes amis," a risky challenge for every tenor, even for a heavyweight like Luciano Pavarotti. By the way . . . do you know how many high C's composer Donizetti packed into this matinee showoff piece? See page 111 for the answer.

Wagner *Contra Mundum*

Throughout his lifetime, Wagner remained a figure of controversy. Some saw him as an artistic messiah, sent to earth to lead the music of the future across the bridge to the ... well, you get the idea. Others thought he was practically the devil incarnate. Both sides were more or less correct.

In the excerpts below, match the invective/comment to the work or its utterer.

1 It's poison—rank poison. All we can make out is an incoherent mass of rubbish, with no more real pretension to be called music than the jangling and clashing of gongs and other uneuphonious instruments . . .

2 It may be that *The Nibelung's Ring* is a very great work, but there has never been anything more tedious and more dragged-out than this rigmarole. In the past, music was supposed to delight people, and now we are tormented and exhausted by it.

3 [It has] too much brass.

4 The overture to *The Mastersingers* is delightful when you know what it is all about; but only those to whom it came as a concert piece without any such clue, and who judged its reckless counterpoint by the standard of Bach . . . can realize how atrocious it used to sound to musicians of the old school.

5 *Siegfried* was abominable. Not a trace of coherent melodies. It would kill a cat and would turn rocks into scrambled eggs from fear of the hideous discords.

6 Not merely polyphonous, but polycacophonous.

7 Wagner is evidently mad.

8 Reminds me of the old Italian painting of a martyr whose intestines are slowly unwound from his body on a reel.

9 So he goes through life, luxuriant, petulant, egoistic, improvident, in everything extreme, roaring, shrieking, weeping, laughing, never doubting himself, never doubting that whoever opposed him, or did not do all for him that he expected, was a monster of iniquity—Wagner *contra mundum*, he always right, the world always wrong.

10 It is a high honor for me to live with the great Master—but it is often beyond bearing!

First the answers, then on to the 20th century!

Answers: Act Two—The 19th Century: Beethoven, Wagner, Tchaikovsky & Verdi

1 A lot more than you think—and none of them performed today.

2 *Der Spiegelritter, Des Teufels Lustschloss, Die Vierjährige Posten, Fernando* (and here you thought that was by ABBA!), *Die Freunde von Salamanka, Die Zwillingsbrüder, Alfonso und Estrella, Die Verschworenen, Fierrabras.*

3 Basically, none, although *Die Zwillingsbrüder* attracted some attention. The title, by the way, means The Twin Brothers.

4 Only one—*Fidelio*—although Beethoven called the opera's earlier versions *Leonore*. Which is why there are three *Leonore* overtures, plus one for *Fidelio*.

5 *Die eheliche Liebe*, or Married Love, which doesn't sound too exciting. *Fidelio* was, of course, Beethoven's first and last opera.

6 That you have to rewrite, rewrite and then rewrite again. Cutting the damn thing doesn't hurt either. *Fidelio* is shorter, tighter and far more dramatically effective than *Leonore*, and it's a shame that more opera composers didn't follow Beethoven's example.

7 None.

8 Not exactly. Carl Maria von Weber's *Die Drei Pintos*, left unfinished at the composer's death, was completed and arranged by Mahler. He was the second famous composer to have a go at the *Pintos*; Meyerbeer had first crack, but passed. It turned out to be not worth the trouble.

9 Chopin, for one. Liszt, for two. Brahms, for three.

10 Well, okay: Liszt did write one opera—*Don Sanche*—which he composed when he was thirteen. Plus he probably had some help from grownups. Does *Don Sanche* still count? Liszt did, however, write plenty of pianistic "paraphrases" on themes from famous operas.

11 Schubert, of course. And Mahler. Hugo Wolf tried his hand at opera in *Der Corregidor* and we all wish he hadn't. Wolf produced a pseudo-Wagnerian mish-mash in which he ripped off two of his own tunes from *Das spanisches Liederbuch*. Brahms was smart enough to leave the musical stage alone.

12 Richard Strauss.

13 I don't.

14 Relax—it's the German word for "songs." The singular form is lied, pronounced "leed."

15 Think of it as the difference between a short story and a novel. There are some writers who can do both, but generally you're either one or the other. Schubert, for example, never found in opera the personal freedom of expression (especially harmonic) that he discovered in song. In fact, there is plenty of evidence that he positively hated the strictures imposed on him by the larger form, and preferred to go his way experimenting with the lied.

16 Gaspare Spontini, remembered today primarily for *La Vestale* (The Vestal Virgin); Luigi Cherubini, whose *Médée* is considered his masterpiece; and Giacomo Meyerbeer, born Jakob Liebmann Meyer Beer in Berlin, who virtually invented the concept of French grand opera. Among his famous works, which to opera were what Andrew Lloyd Webber's musicals are to Broadway today, are *Robert le Diable*, *Les Hugenots*, *Le prophète* and *L'Africaine*.

17 Is Richard Wagner famous enough for you? Wagner came to Paris around 1840 in search of Meyerbeer's blessing. He didn't get it.

18 People have been asking that for a century or so. There were plenty of French composers, such as Daniel Auber, but Meyerbeer overwhelmed everybody else in both reputation and influence. Which is why Wagner, no fool, sought him out.

19 No, Beethoven stayed in Vienna.

20 In a manner of speaking, yes, when Napoleon shelled Vienna.

21 "Ungrateful" means simply that it doesn't lie well for the voice—which means it makes singers look bad, even if they aren't.

22 Take the *Missa Solemnis*. Or the finale of the Ninth Symphony. Please.

23 Not so much lucky as good. In the course of Fidelio/Leonore's many rewrites and rethinks, Beethoven (who was a habitual rewriter in any case) gradually winnowed out the chaff and the dross, leaving only the wheat and the gold, if you follow my metaphors.

24 Leonore, the wife of the imprisoned Florestan, dresses up as a young man named Fidelio and insinuates herself into the service of the jailer, Rocco, in order to free her husband.

25 Marzelline, Rocco's daughter, falls in love with Fidelio.

26 Women disguised as men were a staple of the 18th- and 19th-century adventure tales. *Fidelio* is a "rescue opera"—a type of work particularly favored in France, pointing once again to the influence of French opera on composers of the early 19th century.

27 Mozart's *The Marriage of Figaro* and Richard Strauss's *Der Rosenkavalier* are two of the most famous. Each takes the gender-bending one step further by having a female singer take a male role and then, in the course of the opera, pretend to be a woman.

28 Because, for all its greatness, *Fidelio* encompasses so many different musical styles and moods that it takes a sure hand on the baton to bring the opera into coherent focus.

29 It's impossible to know for sure, but it seems Beethoven began writing one opera and finished up with a very different opera. The light opening domestic scenes for Marzelline and Jacquino could have been composed by Mozart, or at least Haydn, whereas the music turns infinitely darker once we get down inside the jail. Then Wagner's Nibelheim and the spirit kingdom of Keikobad in Strauss's *Die Frau ohne Schatten* are not very far away.

30 Verdi's *La Forza del destino*. Her name is spelled Leonora.

31 "Abscheulicher!" begins the recitative. It basically means, "What a monster!" and then develops into a rip-roaring aria that has the poor soprano not only battling Beethoven's ferocious writing but an army of French horns as well.

32 "Gott, welch' Dunkel hier!" or "My God, it's dark in here!"

33 He's a political prisoner.

34 *Il Prigionero* by Luigi Dallapiccola.

35 No, but he is greedy. His big aria is about gold.

36 A dirty rat named Don Pizarro. Leonore nearly shoots him, but the Minister, Don Fernando, arrives and takes the governor into custody. What happens to him is left to the imagination, but you can bet it isn't good.

37 The story goes that Mahler started it, but in fact it antedates him, being fairly common practice in the 19th century.

38 Yes, *Don Giovanni*. The final scene, in which the principals comment on the punishment of the Don after he is dragged off to Hell by the Statue, was commonly omitted. We know better today.

39 She has to settle for a real boy, Jacquino, and like it. Today she'd probably be in therapy for years and then either become a nun or join a lesbian commune.

40 *Der Freischütz* by Carl Maria von Weber.

41 Richard Wagner's.

42 Heinrich Marschner, composer of *Der Vampyr* and *Hans Heiling*.

43 The famous overture, of course, with its forest-primeval horns. And the supernatural "Wolf's Glen" scene, which did so much to put Wagner on the path to fame and fortune.

44 It is famous — in Germany, where it is often staged. One problem might be its name, which is pretty much untranslatable into English. It means The Free-Shooter, whatever that is. For some reason, it seems clearer in German.

45 You bet: try *Euryanthe* and *Oberon*. Acquired tastes, perhaps, but well worth the trouble.

46 Bel canto—for "beautiful singing."

47 We can start with Rossini, but the heart of the bel canto repertory is the works of Vincenzo Bellini and Gaetano Donizetti.

48 Let's try Bellini's *Norma*, *La Sonnambula* and *I Puritani*; and Donizetti's *Lucia di Lammermoor*, *L'Elisir d'amore*, *La fille du régiment*, *Anna Bolena*, *Roberto Devereux* and *Don Pasquale*.

49 Yes, indeed: it's *Don Pasquale*. Specifically, Ernesto's Act 2-opening aria, "Cercherò lontana terra." And Nino Rota takes the bow!

50 Not if the composer's been dead for a hundred years or so.

51 Donizetti: *Maria di Rohan, Maria Padilla, Maria de Rudenz, Maria Stuarda* (he obviously had a thing for gals named Maria), *Linda di Chamounix, Lucrezia Borgia Emilia di Liverpool* and *Fausta* — and those are just the ones about women! Bellini contributes *Bianca e Fernando, Il pirata, La Straniera, Zaira, Beatrice di Tenda*, among others. He died young.

52 Feel about it any way you like. It's not my cup of tea, owing largely to the static harmonies, which drive me nuts. But I suppose if you were to scratch a real opera fan, you'd find a hard-core bel canto fan. And, boy, do the divas ever get to show off! Which, I suppose, is the whole point . . .

53 Ernest Guiraud, who wrote the recitatives for *Carmen* that, for years, were the standard way to perform what Bizet had intended as spoken dialogue.

54 *Le Roi David, Sylvie, En prison, Le Kobold, Madame Turlupin, Piccolino, Galante aventure* and *Frédégonde*.

55 *Gretna Green.*

56 Offenbach's *Les contes d'Hoffmann.*

57 Saint-Saens.

58 Balakirev, Borodin, Cui, Rimsky-Korsakoff and Mussorgsky.

59 Borodin wrote *Prince Igor*, completed after his death by Rimsky; Mussorgsky wrote *Boris Godunov* and *Khovanschina* (both edited and orchestrated by Rimsky), among others; Rimsky wrote bunches of operas, among them *Sadko*, *The Legend of the Invisible City of Kitezh*, *Mozart and Salieri*, and *The Golden Cockerel*; and Cui, the most obscure of the group, wrote no less than 15 operas, including *William Ratcliff*.

60 It was considered the first Russian nationalist opera. What's odd is that it's based on Heinrich Heine's play about a Scotsman.

61 Glinka.

62 *A Life for the Czar* and *Ruslan and Ludmilla*.

63 *Eugene Onegin* and *The Queen of Spades* (*Pique Dame*).

64 Pushkin, of course. When it came to poetry, Tchaikovsky had good taste.

65 Tchaikovsky adapted *Eugene Onegin* and, together with his brother Modest, *Pique Dame* as well.

66 *Mazepa.*

67 *The Voyevoda, Undine, The Oprichnik, Vakula the Smith, The Maid of Orleans, The Enchantress, Iolanthe.*

68 *Mazepa*—or, *Mazeppa,* a barn-burner of a piano piece by Liszt.

69 *Iolanthe.*

70 *Undine.* E.T.A. Hoffmann, better known as the writer whose life and works inspired Offenbach's *Les contes d'Hoffmann* and *Albert Lortzing.* The water-nymph was a popular gal in the 19th century.

71 *Ivanhoe.* Another non-Gilbert work, *Haddon Hall,* may be termed "light opera."

72 *The Voyevoda.*

73 *The Oprichnik.*

74 *Eugene Onegin.*

75 Calling Dr. Kevorkian! Tchaikovsky died after he foolishly drank some unboiled water in the middle of a cholera epidemic. Whether it was accidental or deliberate has long been a matter for debate. The current thinking is that Tchaikovsky was either forced or encouraged in the fatal draught by a group of noblemen outraged over a homosexual affair he was having with one of their relatives.

76 Shut up and listen, will you?

77 Why, *Il Trovatore*, of course. No other Verdi opera deserves it more.

78 George S. Kaufman, with Morrie Ryskind.

79 Otis B. Driftwood, who spent the picture torturing the snooty Mrs. Claypool (the ineffable Margaret Dumont).

80 Schiller.

81 *I masnadieri* and *Luisa Miller*.

82 It takes place during the Spanish Inquisition, and King Philip II is a major, if offstage, presence.

83 Verdi originally wrote the opera, in French, for the Paris Opera in 1867. But in 1884 he revised it, dropping the first act (although keeping some of the music) and translating it into Italian. Two years later, the so-called Modena Version restored the first act, but maintaining the Italian language. It's fair to say there are three "authentic" versions of *Don Carlo/s*, each one magnificent.

84 French, if you're doing it right. And I'm sure the French would agree!

85 Almost everything, from the radiant beauty of the Fontainebleau act, through the nobility of the Carlos-Posa duet, to the ominous chill of the Grand Inquisitor scene. No major character goes without a scene that befits his or her stature and, from first note to last, Verdi's command of his material would be exceeded only by *Otello*.

86 In my opinion, only one thing: the silly little brass-band march in the *auto-da-fé* scene. It's as if Verdi dug the tune out of his bottom drawer.

87 "Infant" means "prince" in Spanish. Which is what Don Carlos is: a Spanish prince, and the son of King Philip II. He may act like a baby from time to time in the opera, but he isn't one.

88 Not. She's referring to her own beauty, the "fatal gift" that, apparently, no other character in the opera is capable of observing.

89 That's for you to figure out. And it's one of the things that makes this such a wonderful opera.

90 Who knows? At the opera's conclusion, it appears that Carlos is going to have to fight for his life against his father's soldiers and the forces of the Grand Inquisitor. Suddenly, a hand reaches out and draws him into the safety of the monastery at St.-Just. The End.

91 Shakespeare.

92 Arrigo Boito.

93 *Mefistofele.* It was a disaster at its first performances at La Scala.

94 As "Tobia Gorrio," Arrigo Boito was the librettist for Ponchielli's *La gioconda.* Pretty clever, huh?

95 There was a bit of bother about a poem that Boito wrote and with which Verdi took umbrage.

96 *Falstaff.*

97 *King Lear* or, in Italian, *Re Lear.*

98 There's no "th" sound in Italian. Hence *Othello* becomes *Otello.* It certainly sings better that way. Otherwise, the Moor's name would come out sounding like something the kid in *The Music Man* might say.

99 Jago, as in "Iago." Everybody loves a bad guy.

100 Arturo Toscanini.

101 Rossini.

102 Keep reading and you'll find out why.

103 The first, or Venetian, act.

104 The French version by François-Victor Hugo.

105 In the play, she's des-de-MO-na; in the opera, she's des-DAY-mo-na.

106 Iago's "Credo," perhaps the best exposition of sheer villainy in all of opera.

107 Otello both sings and shouts; his wife sings, sings and sings some more. Whereas the slimy Iago conducts his musical dialogue mostly in parlando (speech-song), as if he were not worthy to break out into actual song.

108 *Aida*, of all things.

109 Giuseppina, believe it or not, as Giuseppina Strepponi she had sung Abigaille in the premiere of *Nabucco*.

110 The Casa di Reposo per Musicisti.

111 *Un ballo in maschera*. The original setting was to have been the Sweden of King Gustave III, but since the plot dealt with assassination, the censors made Verdi relocate.

112 Strictly speaking, it means "the woman who has been led astray," which is why we call it *La Traviata*.

113 It means "Viva Vittorio Emanuele, Re d'Italia!" and was a political slogan of the day when Italy was fighting for independence from Austria and, ultimately, unification.

114 The Marchese de Busseto, offered by the King after the premiere of *Falstaff*.

115 Maybe, maybe not. Herr Wagner died six months after little Ricky was born; eight months later, Wagner's mother married Ludwig Geyer, an actor, and Wagner speculated long and hard that his real father might have been Geyer—and, worse, that Geyer might have been Jewish. Assiduous Nazi research into the question of Geyer's paternity, however, assured the Wagner-loving Nazi hierarchy that Geyer was a good Aryan.

116 Mad King Ludwig II of Bavaria.

117 Adolf Hitler, who tried to stage *Die Meistersinger von Nürnberg* with the entire country of Germany as the backdrop, and wound up mounting *Götterdämmerung* instead.

118 Hitler, whose illegitimate father, Alois, had been called by his mother's last name of Schickelgruber until he was formally adopted by the Hitler family, worried that dear old dad was actually the wrong-side-of-the-blanket offspring between his paternal grandmother and the son of a Jewish household in Graz. He was so concerned that he deputized his lawyer, Hans Frank (later Governor-General of Poland) to check it out. Frank thought that the scenario was, in fact, quite likely, but modern scholars like Joachim Fest lean toward simple Alpine incest as the cause of Ms. Schickelgruber's unfortunate condition.

119 Gluck, for his attempt to restore the balance between text and music. Wagner very much considered himself a poet and philosopher as well as a musician.

120 Beethoven.

121 *Die Hochzeit* (The Wedding), *Die Feen* (The Fairies) and *Das Liebesverbot* (The Ban on Love).

122 *Die Novize von Palermo* (The Novice of Palermo).

123 *Rienzi, der Letzte der Tribunen* (Rienzi, the Last of the Tribunes).

124 *The Flying Dutchman*. Wagner and his wife Minna were sailing from Riga, where he was music director of the theater, to Pillau. The ship was forced to drop anchor in Norway.

125 *Tannhäuser*.

126 *Lohengrin*.

127 It's a little gold pinky ring that gives its wearer unlimited power.

128 Technically, it's *Die Walküre*. The first opera, *Das Rheingold*, is actually a prologue ("preliminary evening") to the "three days" of the *Ring* cycle.

129 Considering what happens later, you could say he did, big-time.

130 The latter.

131 *Siegfried*, because he's really old one-eyed Wotan in disguise, and doesn't want anybody to recognize him. Shhhh . . .

132 She wants her sister, Brünnhilde, to promise to give the damn Ring back to the Rhinemaidens.

133 Hagen, who shouts "Zurück vom Ring!" just before the Rhinemaidens drown him.

134 Brittany, Ireland and Cornwall—a regular Celtic love-in.

135 Wagner himself, in the third act of *Die Meistersinger von Nürnberg*, when Hans Sachs tells Eva he knows the story of Tristan and Isolde, and what bad things can happen when an older man falls in love with a younger girl.

136 Albert Lortzing, best known as the composer of *Zar und Zimmermann*.

137 Spain is the setting for *Parsifal*.

138 Jesus of Nazareth and Buddha, among others.

139 True. Near the end of his life, the chronically broke composer (whose opulent lifestyle exceeded even his fame and income) was writing to an American dentist in Leipzig, inquiring about gracing the former Colonies with his presence. One can only wonder what Wagner would have thought of, say, Philadelphia.

140 The *American Centennial March*, which he wrote only for the money. It stinks.

141 The first performance of the *Ring* cycle.

142 Bayreuth. It's pronounced "Buy-royt," not "Bay-root." Beirut is in Lebanon.

143 "Wahnfried" means "Freedom from Delusion."

144 In the backyard of Wahnfried, like a dog.

145 Eduard Hanslick, guyed as Beckmesser in *Die Meistersinger.*

146 *Tannhäuser und der Sängerkrieg auf Wartburg* (Tannhäuser and the Song-Contest on the Wartburg).

147 Because Wagner's libretto derives from two different sources, and he wanted that reflected in the title.

148 Rich gay fan to money-grubbing straight artist, basically. There's no doubt that Ludwig was homosexual, and the uncharitable claim that Wagner and Ludwig had a thing going on—that Wagner was, in effect, a prostitute. But that is to project our prurient sensibility upon another age. Which is something we love doing, but it's still wrong.

149 True.

150 True: as the author of *Jewry in Music*, Wagner was a role model for Adolf Hitler. False: as a composer who knew the best musicians when he saw them, regardless of race or creed, he hired Hermann Levi to conduct *Parsifal*.

151 None.

152 Liszt's daughter, Cosima.

153 Cosima was still married to the pianist and conductor Hans von Bülow at the time.

154 Apparently not: Bülow conducted the premiere of *Tristan und Isolde* two months later. Wagner's son Siegfried was similarly conceived while Cosima and Bülow were still legally man and wife.

Answers: More Name That Tune

1 Tchaikovsky's *Eugene Onegin*.

2 Massenet's *Werther*.

3 Leoncavallo's *Pagliacci*.

4 Benjamin Britten's *Death in Venice*.

5 Monteverdi's *The Coronation of Poppea*.

6 Puccini's *La Bohème*.

Answers: They Won't Sing—Don't Ask Them

1 Prokofiev's *The Fiery Angel*.

2 Mozart's *The Abduction from the Seraglio*.

3 Henze's *Der junge Lord*.

4 Dallapiccola's *Il Prigioniero*.

5 *Regina*, by Marc Blitzstein.

Answers: Who Said It?

1 *b)* Well-known misanthrope and famous missing person Ambrose Bierce, in *The Devil's Dictionary*.

2 *c)* The wasp-tongued Sir Thomas—although it's something one wishes Raft would say to the organ grinder in the famous scene from Howard Hawks' *Scarface.*

3 *a)* Mencken, of course, although the other two guys might just as easily have made the same observation. No opera fan, Mencken also once opined: "The opera is to music what a bawdy house is to a cathedral."

4 *c)* The great Galli-Curci, who ought to have known. Or known better.

5 *a)* The great and cranky art critic Ruskin, extremely cheesed-off by a performance of Wagner's *Die Meistersinger.*

6 All three. Twain also famously observed that "Wagner's music is not as bad as it sounds," which may or may not have been a compliment.

7 *c)* Shaw, who was speaking about Gounod's *La Rédemption.* Shaw was a Mozart and Wagner kind of guy.

8 *c)* Wagner, who certainly practiced what he preached.

9 *b)* Shaw, of course.

10 *a)* Nietzsche, in *The Twilight of the Gods*; formerly, Nietzsche had been one of Wagner's strongest supporters. The fact that he died insane has nothing to do with any of the foregoing.

11 *a)* Wilde, in *The Picture of Dorian Gray.*

12 *b)* Sir Walter Scott, *Marmion.*

Answers: Wagner *Contra Mundum*

1 *Lohengrin,* according to an anonymous London critic in 1855.

2 Tchaikovsky.

3 *Lohengrin* again. This time the critic was Wagner himself.

4 George Bernard Shaw, actually paying Wagner a compliment.

5 Richard Strauss, who later recanted.

6 *Tannhäuser.* That London critic again.

7 Hector Berlioz.

8 *Tristan und Isolde,* courtesy of Eduard "Beckmesser" Hanslick.

9 Ernest Newman, Wagner's biographer and ardent admirer.

10 Not Cosima, as you might think, but Hans von Bülow.

Answers: Act Two Photo Captions

1 Pages 70–71, 82–83: Katia Ricciarelli, José Carreras, Luciano "Lucky" Pavarotti and Giacomo Aragall (left foreground), with Mama Aragall watching.

2 Page 78: Sarah Tucker's sister Kathy was married to John Pierce.

3 Page 86: No less than nine.

Opposite: Birgit Nilsson in *Elektra*

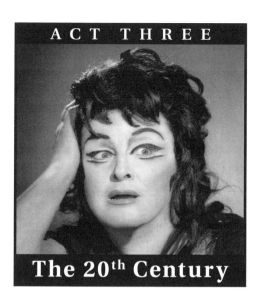

ACT THREE

The 20th Century

Berg, Puccini & Strauss

Yes, I know that to some people the very
words "20th-century music" have a terrifying
connotation, all sound and fury that signifies
nothing—or very, very little. But don't worry: 20th-
century opera really isn't as bad as it sounds. Just ask
Mark Twain, or Wagner, or somebody.

To prove it, let's start with one of those odd little
historical coincidences that you can use to amaze your
friends and discomfit your enemies:

1 From which Shakespearean play, also a Verdi opera, did we lift a phrase in the first sentence on page 113?

2 Which two strikingly dissimilar operas, both staples of the repertory and among the greatest operas of the century, were premiered within four months of each other? (Hint: the weirder one came first.)

3 Name the composers.

4 How many other operas did each of these men write? Enumerate them, in order.

5 Isn't there a typographical error in there somewhere?

6 Isn't there another 20th-century German opera that's more or less a blatant rip-off of Berg's first opera?

Yes, friends, we're talking about Berg and Puccini. And if it seems odd to link those composers in the same sentence, well, that just proves how diverse and rich the operatic music of the 20th century is (or was).

For the music of these two great composers—the one a neurasthenic Austrian, the other a sybaritic Italian—pretty much foreshadows all that comes after them. For all the hullabaloo of the succeeding 75 years, most 20th-century operas have fallen into one of the two camps. So learn about Berg and Puccini and you're more than half-way to understanding the whole of modern opera.

Let's start with Berg:

7 Of which school was Berg a member?

8 To which earlier school does this name refer?

9 Who else was in the second school?

10 Which one of their names is spelled with an umlaut?

11 Which one of them used to be a "von"?

12 What happened to him, fatal-accident-wise?

13 True or false: Schoenberg once had his portrait painted by George Gershwin.

14 True or false: early Webern pieces sort of sound like Mahler.

15 True or false: early Schoenberg pieces sound like Wagner.

16 True or false: most Berg pieces sound like Mahler and Wagner.

17 True or false: all this music sounds like the noise that something the cat dragged in might make *in extremis*.

Berg's first opera, *Wozzeck*, is famous (some would say notorious) for its alleged atonality or downright twelve-tonality. What about these charges—which to a lover of traditional Italian opera (e.g., Puccini) are tantamount to treason?

18 Name the avant-garde playwright upon whose play *Wozzeck* is based.

19 In which year was this quintessentially 20th-century study of proletarian anomie written?

20 I hear *Wozzeck* is a twelve-tone opera. Is this true?

21 What is twelve-tone music?

22 Who invented twelve-tone music anyway?

23 Why?

24 Well, is *Wozzeck* a tonal opera, then?

25 Then it must be atonal, right?

26 Name the twelve-tone scene in *Wozzeck*.

27 Name the famous tonal interlude in *Wozzeck*.

28 Each act of *Wozzeck* is a distinct musical form. Describe the opera's unique structure, act by act and, if possible, scene by scene.

29 Is there anything in *Wozzeck* that sounds more or less like opera as we know it?

30 So why do some folks, to this day, still walk out when *Wozzeck* is performed down at their neighborhood opera house?

Berg's other opera, *Lulu*, is everything its name implies: a real lulu of an opera. It's got everything a self-respecting opera needs: exhibitionism, lust, rape, fornication, adultery, lesbianism, prostitution, murder. Hell, *Lulu* is a family-values festival! Let's check the *Lulu* tote board and see how the fabulous babe stacks up:

31 Name the opera Berg was going to compose after *Wozzeck*, but abandoned in favor of *Lulu*. (Hint: Schoenberg also considered setting the story.)

32 Which major German-language playwright wrote the play upon which it would have been based?

33 The libretto of *Lulu* is based on which two plays?

34 By which playwright?

35 Berg died before finishing the orchestration of *Lulu*. What killed him?

36 Who finally did complete the orchestration, and when?

37 In which year was the full score of *Lulu* finally heard, where was it performed, and who conducted it?

38 How many people either have, or attempt to have, or desire to have, sex with Lulu during the course of the opera?

Berg was not the only member of the Second Viennese School to write opera. Which naturally begs the questions . . .

39 Who else in the Second Viennese School tried his hand at opera?

40 Name his operas.

As good as *Erwartung* is (*Moses und Aron* has its adherents, but in its unfinished state it makes a better spectacle than an opera, especially the bit with the naked virgins), there can be little doubt that Berg deserves pride of place among the serialist composers of the first half of the 20th century. But there was another great German opera composer, a contemporary of Berg, who looms even larger in the operatic repertory.

41 Name him.

Yes, Strauss. The Bavarian Strauss, that is, not to be confused with Johann Strauss Sr. or Jr., the waltz kings of old Vienna. The Strauss of the great tone poems and the great songs and the great operas, whose long life spanned everything from the Kaiser to Hitler to the American Zone of Occupation. The Strauss who was a celebrated musician under the Double Eagle and under the swastika as well. Oh yes, and under the Stars and Stripes. *That* Strauss.

42 Where was Strauss born?

43 What is that city's most famous export?

44 What was Strauss's familial connection to that famous export?

45 Hans von Bülow, the great Wagnerian cuckold, called the young Strauss "Richard the Third." Why?

46 In addition to being a great composer, Strauss was also a great conductor. Which famous children's opera was given its world premiere under his baton at Weimar? (Hint: it was also the first Metropolitan Opera radio broadcast.)

47 Why was the small city of Weimar such an important arts center?

48 Name the two other great musical cities where Strauss led the local opera company.

49 With whom did Strauss share the musical directorship of the latter company?

50 Like many a composer/conductor before him, Strauss married one of his singers. Name her.

51 Like many a composer/conductor before him, Strauss's wife turned out to be something of (ahem!) a harridan. Name another great composer whose little wifey was less than a loving helpmeet.

52 Strauss got his revenge on Pauline in a number of musical ways. Name one Strauss tone poem and two Strauss operas that depict the blissful, loving atmosphere of the Strauss family household.

(continued on page 121)

Savoy-Faire

As everybody knows, Sir Arthur Sullivan was a prolific opera and operetta composer, both in partnership with W.S. Gilbert and with others. A peculiarity of Sullivan's operas, though, is that most of them have alternative titles. Just as Mozart's *Don Giovanni* is really called *Il dissoluto punito*, most of Sullivan's operas have alternate titles. OK, Savoyards: match 'em up.

1 *The Gods Grow Old*

2 *The Lass That Loved a Sailor*

3 *Bunthorne's Bride*

4 *The Slave of Duty*

5 *Castle Adamant*

6 *The Law of the Ladrones*

7 *The Long-Lost Brothers*

8 *The Town of Titipu*

9 *The Peer and the Peri*

10 *The Merryman and His Maid*

11 *The Witch's Curse*

12 *The King of Barataria*

13 *The Flowers of Progress*

14 *The Statutory Duel*

15 *The Story-Teller and the Slave*

16 *The Caves of Carrig-Cleena*

(continued from page 119)

Strauss is considered one of the century's leading opera composers. He is also regarded, quite rightly, as one of the finest composers of orchestral tone poems who ever lived. But there's something odd about the way in which he went about writing in both genres.

53 What was it?

54 Like Wagner, Strauss composed a couple of duds before finding his stride. Name them.

55 Did you say, "Foyer-snot"?

56 And then he wrote a real opera, right?

57 Which was based upon which play by which famous playwright?

58 Which was translated into German from the original what?

59 After which Strauss turned his attention to?

60 With a libretto by which Austro-German playwright, and based upon which ancient Greek?

61 Strauss and this fellow together wrote a number of operas together. How many and which ones?

62 True or false: Strauss's late operas aren't a patch on his earlier ones.

63 If not, why not?

The collapse of Strauss from the dazzling musical impresario of *Ariadne auf Naxos* to the bathetic bore of *Die Liebe der Danae* is one of music's most mysterious occurrences. A famous contemporary, who was certainly no Strauss fan, called him "the talent that was once a genius."

64 Name the purveyor of this particular *bon mot*.

65 Name another talent that was never quite a genius, but whose opera *Palestrina* enjoyed a certain vogue in the early part of the century.

66 Who, what or where is Palestrina?

67 Another German composer chose a medieval painter as the subject for an opera. Name the composer, the subject and the opera.

68 Are these operas any good, and if so why aren't they performed more often?

But, fortunately for opera, Strauss had an Italian contemporary whose works were far more consistent across the length of his career. I'm speaking, of course, about Giacomo Puccini.

Ever since a famous musicologist called *Tosca* "a shabby little shocker," it has been fashionable to deride Puccini's gifts, especially in academic circles.

69 Who was he?

Real musicians, however, will have none of this nonsense. And a glance at any Puccini score will show you how far wrong that assessment is. Puccini was not only a master of orchestration (I think one reason he's looked at askance is that his scores sound so damn good) but a master melodist and an outstanding musical dramatist as well. Almost unfailingly, Puccini was able to match the music to the moment, with the result that he is the last in the line of composers whose works figure regularly in the operatic repertoire. Indeed, it's hard to imagine an opera season without ol' Giacomo. By any measure, Puccini's works form a major branch of the Italian repertory—and that's still the repertory that sells tickets. A world without Puccini would be a poorer place indeed.

70 Puccini is often regarded as the natural successor to Verdi. But there is another Italian composer, a one-hit wonder, who influenced him far more. Name him.

71 Name his opera.

72 What does its title mean?

Oddly, Puccini had a strong connection to the U.S. So let's start with some questions about Puccini and the country named after his countryman, Amerigo Vespucci.

73 Which Puccini opera takes place in the U.S.A.?

74 On which play by which playwright was it based?

75 How did Puccini encounter it, and in what form?

76 So how did he understand what it was about?

77 How did Puccini himself refer, in shorthand, to this opera?

78 What personal unpleasantness caused Puccini to interrupt his work on this opera?

79 Did this surprise anybody?

80 Where and when was this opera premiered, and by which famous conductor?

81 Before he started work on this opera, what was Puccini considering as a subject?

82 Which other Puccini opera ends in the good old U.S. of A.?

83 Name some other American characters found in Puccini's operas.

84 In *The Girl of the Golden West* there are two American Indian characters. Name them.

85 Which other Puccini opera was premiered in the U.S., where, and when?

(continued on page 130)

Now this is an easy one. We tell you that this is the chorus of the Metropolitan Opera in a rehearsal for Cavalleria rusticana *by Pietro Mascagni; you only have to name the one gentleman who does not belong on stage. . . . Answer on page 169.*

Yet More Name That Tune

1 We're pitching this turnarounder for the art-house aesthetes who gobble up downer endings with their popcorn. Miserable GI (Gary Oldman) is shacking up with a cheap hooker (Jennifer Jason Leigh) and their kid when she falls for a fancy-pants drum major and gives our hero the old heave-ho-ski. Natch, he's pissed; he's also crazier than a bedbug. And so the schmuck takes his revenge on the dame, cutting her up O.J.-style before drowning himself in a handy lake. Costa-Gavras is already on board to helm. (Memo: make sure there's *plenty* of sex, esp. in the Euro-version.)

2 Paging Sir Richard Attenborough to Remake Heaven! In a prequel to *Gandhi*, the holy Mahatma (Ben Kingsley) takes on a corrupt South African regime while learning to spin cloth and sharpen up his philosophy of nonviolence. Rewrite is already penciling in a couple of massacres for the action crowd, but otherwise we think we've got a high-toned big-budget winner on our hands—and come springtime we're sure the Academy will agree!

3 Russ Meyer fans, please copy: this one's about a gal and her two best friends (if you get my meaning). The hook is, she's tired of being a girl and would enjoy being a boy. So her bazooms simply float away into the sky and off she goes. Meanwhile hubby comes home, thinks she's been kidnapped—and (yesssss!) puts on her dress. And promptly gives birth to 40,000 kids in a single day! Needless to say, we're thinking one of those avant-garde French *auteurs* like Luc Besson for this one. But we do like Kevin Kline and Phoebe Cates for the leads. Get a load of the Grand Tetons on that one!

4 It will take a Quentin Tarantino to keep all the rewrites straight, but here goes: rough, tough tyrant (Bob Hoskins in his best *Long Good Friday* mode) takes over the Kremlin and promptly sets off a killer war with (OK, so this takes a little stretch) the Poles, led by a guy named the false Dmitri (I don't get it, but somebody must) and a dame named Marina (Meryl Streep, packing her to-die-for Polish accent). There's pageantry, romance, treachery and real horasho violence as the usurper tries desperately to hang on to his crown in the face of overwhelming odds. The costumes alone will cost a fortune, but the budget's got to be up there on the screen. Where's Edith Head when we need her?

5 Too bad DeMille's pushing up daisies, because here's one that would have had Chuck Heston roaring out of retirement. Moses (you-know-who) and his bad-ass bro' Aron (Lee Marvin? Dick Widmark? Who's still alive?) duel over who carries the bigger stick (if you know what I mean!) with the Israelites. We love these religious epics because you can put in all the sex and nudity you want and still stay on the right side of the Moral Majority! Like the orgy

scene from Act 2 where four naked virgins get slaughtered by high priests right in the middle of the old *je ne sais quoi*! (Memo: tell Ken Russell to stop calling. We'll call him.)

6 The Greeks had a word for it: boffo! Super-classy libretto goes right back to Homer, er, Sophocles for this electric tale of matricide-o-mania! We start with an ax murder in a bathtub for back story (Memo: see how high Paul Haggis's rate is these days)—and it just keeps on getting better, culminating in some serious chop-socky in a multi-mayhem finale that'll have the teenagers screaming for more. John Carpenter directs, and Jessica Simpson plays the damsel in distress. Personally, I like Harvey Fierstein for Aegisthus, but I could be wrong.

Real People

Operas written about historical personages—or, more recently, still-living or just recently deceased people—have long been with us. For each real person listed below, name the opera or operas in which he or she figures prominently as a character.

1 Richard Nixon.

2 Marie Duplessis.

3 Nero.

4 Edgar Allan Poe.

5 El Cid.

6 William Tell.

7 King Gustave III of Sweden.

8 Jack the Ripper.

9 Peter the Great.

10 A neurology patient of Dr. Oliver Sacks.

11 Leon Klinghoffer.

12 Publius Cornelius Scipio Aemilianus.

13 Joan of Arc.

14 Eva Perón.

15 Lucretia Borgia.

16 Susan B. Anthony.

17 Mohandas K. Gandhi.

18 Hans Sachs.

19 George Gordon, Lord Byron.

20 Attila the Hun.

21 Queen Elizabeth I.

22 John Bunyan.

23 Nebuchadnezzar.

24 Marilyn Monroe.

25 Peter the Great.

26 William Tell.

27 Christopher Columbus.

28 Duke Bluebeard.

29 Walther von der Vogelweide.

30 Albert Einstein.

(continued from page 124)

Puccini's most famous opera, of course, is La Bohème. But he is not the only composer to have tackled that particular subject.

86 Name another Italian composer who, in direct competition with Puccini, wrote a *La Bohème*.

87 His *Bohème* wasn't such a success, but he did have one big hit. Name it.

88 No matter who's composing it, where is *La Bohème* set?

Let's take a look at the Puccini operas, in order, with a question or two about each:

89 Who or what are the Willis (*Le villi*)?

90 Where is *Edgar* set?

91 Who wrote the first draft of the libretto of *Manon Lescaut*?

92 Which famous opera was given its Italian premiere in Turin, just before Puccini's *La Bohème*?

93 For a time, Puccini gave up on *Tosca* and ceded the rights to another composer. Who was he?

94 Puccini's original notion for *Madama Butterfly*, later discarded, was to set the first act where?

95 The opening-night cast for *La Fanciulla del West* was of all-star caliber. Name the stars.

96 *La rondine* was originally intended for which opera house?

97 Who conducted the premiere of *Il Trittico*?

98 Name the three operas that make up the "triptych."

99 What other famous composer wrote an opera called *Turandot*?

(continued on page 134)

Farewell for La Divina. Maria Callas after her last recital in New York's Carnegie Hall.
What year did she call it a career? *Turn to page 169 for the answer.*

(continued from page 131)

As we have seen, one name often associated with Puccini is that of Arturo Toscanini. When it came time for the maestro to name his three children, however, he drew inspiration from the works of another, much more obscure, Italian opera composer.

100 What were Toscanini's children's names?

101 Who was the composer?

102 Name his most famous opera.

103 Besides their operatic origin, what's unusual about the children's names?

104 What's so strange about that?

105 Which famous musician did one of Toscanini's daughters marry?

106 And what was odd about that?

At his death in 1924, Puccini left his last opera, *Turandot*, unfinished. Its premiere, conducted of course by Toscanini, was made possible because one of Puccini's students finished it. Whether he did a very good job or not is open to question.

107 What was the student's name?

108 And did he do a very good job?

109 Name a couple of his other operas.

110 What was Toscanini's reaction?

111 So are we stuck with it?

With the death of Puccini and of Berg a decade later, 20th-century opera seemed poised for a spurt of new development. Waiting in the wings to take over the Puccinian mantle was Gian Carlo Menotti, while the serialists, who were busily propagating themselves in the academies of both Europe and America, appeared to offer a number of worthy successors. And what happened?

112 Well, what did happen?

Yes, the Russians. And one of them in particular energized the genre—but at great personal and professional cost. Let's take a quick look at the marvelous Russkies, and what they wrought, especially between the wars.

113 Which famous composers were denounced by Stalin during the infamous purges?

114 Which one of them really was in danger of his life for a time?

115 Why? Which opera pushed the Leader and Teacher over the edge?

116 What did *Pravda* call it?

117 What happened then?

118 And is this such a bad thing?

119 So was *Lady Macbeth* a total loss? I thought it came back in bowdlerized form later on. What was it called?

120 What frosted Uncle Joe so?

121 What is the name of Shostakovich's first opera?

122 Is it worse or better than *Lady Macbeth*?

123 True or false: *Lady Macbeth* is based on a play by Shakespeare.

124 The chilling effect brought on by Stalin's foray into music criticism affected another Soviet composer, who spent nearly a quarter-century working on his operatic masterpiece. Name the composer and the opera.

One Russian-born composer, however, wasn't affected by Stalinism—for the simple reason that he had left the Motherland long before, and was living in Switzerland and, later, the U.S.

125 Who was he?

126 His first opera owes a great deal to the music of his teacher, as well as the fables of Hans Christian Andersen. Name the opera and name the teacher.

127 Where would Russian composers be without Pushkin? Name his opera based on a Pushkin text.

128 Many 20th-century composers have tackled the Oedipus myth. Name this composer's opera on the subject and its librettist, along with three other modern Oedipus operas.

129 His most famous, and widely performed, opera is based on a series of engravings by which famous British artist?

130 Who wrote the libretto?

(continued on page 141)

Who Am I?

You'll know a real opera fan by the way he or she can toss off the names of even the most minor characters in a given work.

Here's a baker's dozen of opera babes—So name 'em, already, plus the opera in which they appear:

1 The saucy little serving wench, whose party-minded machinations land her horny employer in jail.

2 King Phillip II's desperate housewife.

3 Despite the opera's title, she's really from India.

4 The hapless Gibichung gal.

5 The seductive sorceress who's a far cry from Azucena.

6 Gianni Schicchi's daughter in Puccini's *Prizzi's Honor*—oops, *Gianni Schicchi.*

7 The first and last names of Mozart's Countess and in what way she is related to the barber of Seville.

8 Veit Pogner's daughter.

9 The only lady in the Borough who's nice to the weird fisherman with an unhealthy interest in little boys.

10 A lady of the evening, afloat on a gondola, with a song on her lips.

11 Alone by a wishing well and looking for her lost crown.

12 A lost handkerchief is prelude to a fatal kiss.

13 Death in a gunny sack, courtesy of dear old dad.

For the distaff side's ogling pleasure, a dozen-plus primo *uomos.*

14 Gutrune's full, and Hagen's half, brother.

15 Hans Sachs's apprentice.

16 A leading man for both Puccini and Massenet, but not a hero.

17 Double G dad spells double trouble for poor Al and Vi.

18 Thrashed by Mozart's Don.

19 The monk, the priest and the prince in *Boris Godunov*.

20 The hero of *The Pilgrim's Progress*.

21 Hubby of Katarina, soon to be late.

22 A monkey of a young English nobleman.

23 Annina is his partner in crime.

24 The famous explorer, sailor and Meyerbeerian hero.

25 The brother of the heroine of the opera the Germans call *Gretchen*.

26 A Mozartian chief panjandrum who can't sing a lick.

Who was the tenor who accompanied la prima donna assoluta on her final tour? See page 169 for the answer.

(continued from page 137)

To my ears, Prokofiev's operas are nowhere near as accomplished as Shostakovich's. The fabled *War and Peace* is almost as long as the novel, while the allegedly humorous *The Love for Three Oranges* is only allegedly humorous.

131 Name the American opera company that gave *Oranges* its world premiere.

Still, Prokofiev managed to muster one stunning opera: *The Fiery Angel*. Like most great operas, it's about . . .

132 Sex?

But more than that, it's one of the frankest displays of neurotic female sexuality ever penned. Based on a historical novel by Valery Bryussov, it's the story of Renata (an impossible to sing role that's even more impossible to sing than most impossible to sing roles), a woman who's convinced that her special angel, Madiel, has been making love to her for years in the human form of Count Heinrich. (The fact that the opera takes place in 16th-century Cologne doesn't help Renata to get the kind of psychiatric care she so obviously needs.) She pours out her heart to one Knecht Ruprecht—

133 Who?

Who, of course, immediately falls in love with her. The pair finally hunts down Heinrich, who spurns Renata. Ruprecht challenges Heinrich to a duel, but when Renata sees Heinrich bathed in light, she again believes him to be her Fiery Angel and begs Ruprecht not to hurt him. This naturally leads to Ruprecht's being badly wounded, and Renata feels just terrible about it. Not enough to marry the poor schnook, however: Renata joins a convent, Ruprecht falls under the influence of Mephistopheles his own bad self, and at the end, drags Renata off to torture, death and hellfire and damnation right under the nose of the Inquisition. Some fun, huh?

134 In modern opera, convents are no safe havens a la *The Sound of Music*. Renata goes to hell, and Suor Angelica's sins come back to haunt her. But the greatest convent opera of them all was written by a Frenchman. Name the composer and his opera.

Twentieth-century opera is not all gloom and doom, though. Take, for example:

135 The delightful one-act opera whose cast of characters includes a Chinese Cup, a Cat, an Armchair, a Grandfather Clock and a Tea Pot.

136 On a story by which *en vogue* French writer was this opera based?

137 The same composer wrote another comic one-act opera in which a grandfather clock offers an unexpected place of refuge. Name it.

Meanwhile, across the Channel in Britain, opera composers were finally awakening from their centuries-long, post-Purcell slumber. Indeed, the rise of British opera was one of the happiest developments of the mid-to-late 20th century. Composers such as Frederick Delius, William Walton, Michael Tippett and Harrison Birtwistle have revitalized the genre. But the one whose works deserve the most stage time, it seems to me, is . . .

138 The British composer whose operas included adaptations of Synge, Bunyan and Shakespeare.

Yes, RVW, after Elgar the most influential of the mid-century Britons and a composer whose works, alas, are not heard often enough in either American symphony halls or opera houses. Let's correct the widespread ignorance about "Rafe":

139 Name the Vaughan Williams symphony and opera that share several musical themes.

140 This opera turned out to be a warm-up for *The Pilgrim's Progress*.

141 RVW once joked that in writing this particular opera, he wished to put a boxing match on the stage at Covent Garden. Name it.

142 The terrible beauty of the Irish coast was never invoked more feelingly than in this one-act opera.

143 Of which of his operas, a failure at its premiere, did the composer say, "It's not like the operas they are used to, but it's the sort of opera I wished to write, and there it is."

144 This opera, by one of RVW's contemporaries and countrymen, takes place on "a plantation on the Mississippi in Louisiana." Name the opera and the composer.

145 And, speaking of plantations, this opera, by an early 20th-century American, takes place on the outskirts of Texarkana, Arkansas.

(continued on page 145)

A + B = C: Musical Equations

No artist creates in a vacuum. Every great composer, no matter how original, builds on the works of his forebears, borrowing a little, adding a little and passing the whole thing off to his artistic descendants. Complete the follow musical equations by following the example below. Watch out: they're tricky!

If Haydn + Mozart = Beethoven, then

1 Schoenberg + Mahler + Wagner – Webern = ?

2 J.C. Bach + G.F. Handel ÷ Salieri = ?

3 Handel + Schumann – Chopin = ?

4 Gluck + Beethoven + Weber = ?

5 Bellini + Clementi = ?

6 Chopin + Thalberg + Wagner = ?

7 Donizetti + Rossini – Puccini = ?

8 Scarlatti + Rimsky-Korsakoff + Milhaud – Schoenberg = ?

9 Beethoven + Ravel = ?

10 Mozart + Joachim Raff = ?

11 Mozart + Brahms + Mussorgsky = ?

12 Beethoven + Brahms – Mozart = ?

13 Puccini + Saint-Saens – Gounod = ?

14 Leoncavallo + Mascagni + Verdi = ?

15 John Philip Sousa + Schubert + Bellini = ?

16 Puccini + Bellini – Stravinsky = ?

17 John Cage + Nadia Boulanger – Boulez = ?

18 Wagner + Mahler + Bruckner = ?

19 Glinka + Borodin + Balakirev – Tchaikovsky = ?

20 Zemlinsky + Webern – Berg = ?

(continued from page 143)

Which brings us to the works of RVW's successor as the leading composer in Britain, a man whose name just happened to be Britten. Let's check him out:

146 Which Benjamin Britten opera is set in the U.S.A.?

147 Which opera is based on a story by Herman Melville?

148 Which opera is based on a ghost story?

149 In which Britten opera is a man crowned Queen of the May?

150 The "Sea Interludes" are from which opera?

151 This opera was influenced by the Japanese Noh plays.

152 A Munich writer is the doomed hero of this one.

153 An opera fit for a queen.

154 "The ceremony of innocence is drowned."

155 This opera was written for television.

156 Writing an opera for television was not as unusual as we might think today. Name the Stravinsky and Menotti operas that were likewise composed for the tube.

Another modern British composer is Oliver Knussen. His best-known stage work is based on (you could look it up) a children's book.

157 Name the opera, the book and the book's author and illustrator.

And while we're at it, let's take a look at some other national schools as well.

158 Which great Czech composer wrote an opera whose formal title is "Her Stepdaughter," and under what name is this work performed?

159 The works of the Belgian symbolist poet Maurice Maeterlinck resulted in two operas. Name them.

160 In which opera is the heroine 337 years old?

161 In which opera is the leading man "a cripple"?

162 Who wrote an opera about a telephone conversation?

163 Who is the Saint of Bleecker Street?

164 Name the opera whose hero is an Egyptian pharaoh.

165 This was dubbed the "topless opera" at its Washington premiere in 1967. Why? Name it and its composer.

166 This Czech opera is about a bagpipe player.

167 This opera was written to accompany a silent movie directed by Jean Cocteau.

168 This cycle of operas is called "The Seven Days of the Week." Who wrote it?

169 This one, by a contemporary Italian composer, is a Faust opera based not on Goethe but on the novel by Thomas Mann.

170 This opera, by another modern Italian, is called simply *Opera*. Name the composer.

And finally, while we're on the subject,

171 What does the word "opera" mean, anyway?

Answers: Act Three—The 20th Century: Berg, Puccini & Strauss

1 From *Macbeth*, we appropriated "sound and fury," also the title of a great Faulkner novel.

2 *Wozzeck* (December 1925) and *Turandot* (April 1926).

3 Alban Berg and Giacomo Puccini.

4 Berg, one (*Lulu*); Puccini, eleven: *Le Villi* (*The Willies*—really!), *Edgar*, *Manon Lescaut*, *La Bohème*, *Tosca*, *Madama Butterfly*, *La Fanciulla del West*, *La rondine*, and *Il Trittico* (consisting of three one-act operas, *Il Tabarro*, *Suor Angelica* and *Gianni Schicchi*).

5 Yes, in *Wozzeck*. It was supposed to be *Woyzeck*, like the play.

6 Yes, Bernd Alois Zimmermann's *Die Soldaten* (The Soldiers).

7 The Second Viennese School.

8 The First Viennese School, consisting mainly of Haydn and Mozart, who had no idea they were attending a school. They thought they were writing music for various crowned heads in order to make a living. The Second Viennese laddies knew better.

9 Arnold Schoenberg, the founder; and Anton Webern, like Berg, a disciple.

10 Neither. Schoenberg, who might have used an umlaut over the "o," spelled it out instead.

11 That would be Webern, who dropped the nobiliary particle the way Schoenberg eschewed his umlaut.

12 He was shot by an American soldier in September 1945 when he stepped outside his son-in-law's residence for a smoke after curfew.

13 True. Gershwin was an accomplished portrait painter, limning—among others—himself and Edward G. Robinson.

14 True. *Im Sommerwind*, for example.

15 True again. Think of *Verklärte Nacht*.

16 True once more, if you throw in a little Schoenberg.

17 False.

18 Georg Büchner.

19 1837, believe it or not. Büchner was ahead of his time.

20 No. Only one scene is composed in the twelve-tone style.

21 A system of composing in which all twelve notes of the chromatic scale are deemed to be equal, and none can be repeated before all twelve are sounded. In theory this musical egalitarianism is swell, but audiences, perversely, went on preferring music that was in the key of Something.

22 Berg's teacher, mentor and friend, Arnold Schoenberg.

23 Because he could.

24 Sort of.

25 You could say that, given that it has no key signatures and only a few fixed key centers. But, when all is sung and done, it doesn't *sound* atonal.

26 Act 1, Scene 4 (the Passacaglia).

27 The last interlude, an elegy for the drowned protagonist, which is composed in D minor.

28 Act 1, Five Character Pieces: Suite, Rhapsody, Military March and Lullaby, Passacaglia, and Rondo; Act 2, Symphony in Five Movements: Sonata Movement, Fantasia and Fugue, Largo, Scherzo, Rondo con introduzione; Act 3, Six Inventions: Invention on a Theme, on a Note, on a Rhythm, on a Six-Note Chord, on a Key (interlude), on a Regular Quaver Motion.

29 You bet: Marie's lullaby, for example. Not to mention all the little waltzes, marches, hunting songs and polkas that dot the score.

30 I don't know. I do know, however, they're missing a good show.

31 *Und Pippa tanzt!* (*And Pippa dances!*).

32 Gerhart Hauptmann.

33 *Erdgeist* (Earth-Spirit) and *Die Büchse der Pandora* (Pandora's Box).

34 Frank Wedekind.

35 A bee sting, basically.

36 Friedrich Cerha, in 1974.

37 In 1979, at the Paris Opera. Pierre Boulez was the conductor.

38 I count, fittingly, twelve: the Painter, who tries to rape her; her husband, the Medical Specialist, who dies when he encounters the Painter and Lulu *in flagrante*; Dr. Schön, her lover and patron; the Prince, who wants to take her away with him to Africa; the Acrobat and the Schoolboy, two of her admirers; Alwa, Schön's son; the Countess Geschwitz, a lesbian; the Marquis, who wants to sell her into white slavery in a Cairo brothel; and her three clients at the end of the opera, when she is working as a prostitute—the Professor, the Negro, and Jack the Ripper.

39 Only Schoenberg. Webern gave opera a pass.

40 *Erwartung, Die glückliche Hand, Von Heute auf Morgen, Moses und Aron.*

41 Richard Strauss.

42 In Munich.

43 Beer.

44 His mother was a member of the Pschorr family, one of Munich's major breweries. Still is. The brewery, that is.

45 Because, as the ever-faithful von B. pointed out, "after Wagner, there can be no Richard the Second." People really thought and talked like that before World War I, when they still believed that art mattered.

46 Humperdinck's *Hänsel und Gretel.*

47 Because Goethe lived there. And Schiller. And Liszt. And Wagner. And Strauss. Not all at the same time, of course.

48 Munich and Vienna.

49 Franz Schalk.

50 Pauline von Ahna.

51 Franz Haydn, whose missus sometimes used his scores for cleaning up household spills.

52 *Symphonia Domestica; Die Frau ohne Schatten* (The Dyer's Wife) and *Intermezzo* (Christine).

53 He wrote most of his tone poems first, then dropped the form and wrote most of his operas.

54 *Guntram* and *Feursnot.*

55 I did not. The name of the opera, which means "Fire Famine" (whatever *that* means), is pronounced "foyers-note." So there.

56 *Salome.*

57 *Salome* by Oscar Wilde, believe it or not.

58 From the original French.

59 *Elektra.*

60 Hugo von Hofmannsthal, based on his own play, after Sophocles.

61 Six: *Elektra, Der Rosenkavalier, Ariadne auf Naxos, Die Frau ohne Schatten, Die ägyptische Helena, Arabella.*

62 Despite the best efforts of late-Strauss partisans such as John Crosby of the Santa Fe Opera, true. I don't wish anyone to have to sit through *The Egyptian Helen* or *Daphne,* especially on an empty stomach, or in the rain.

63 Because, for all their masterful construction, Strauss's later works lack the two important ingredients that make his earlier operas so wonderful: Hofmannsthal's sharply observed libretti and Strauss's gift for melody. There's plenty of melody in the later works. It's just not very good.

64 Stravinsky, who ought to have known, since he could have made the same observation about himself.

65 Hans Pfitzner.

66 Giovanni Pierluigi da Palestrina was a great composer of the Italian renaissance.

67 Paul Hindemith's *Mathis der Maler*, about the life of the 16th-century painter Mathias Grünewald.

68 You can see *Mathis* or *Palestrina* with some regularity—if you live in Germany. Otherwise, forget it. They don't travel very well.

69 Joseph Kerman.

70 Amilcare Ponchielli.

71 *La Gioconda*.

72 The Ballad Singer, more or less.

73 *La Fanciulla del West*—or should we say *The Girl of the Golden West*?

74 *The Girl of the Golden West*, by David Belasco.

75 He saw it in English while in New York in 1907 for the Metropolitan Opera premieres of *Manon Lescaut* and *Madama Butterfly*. Puccini did not speak English.

76 He read it later in Italian translation.

77 As *"la Girl,"* or *"mia Girl."*

78 The suicide of a serving girl, who killed herself after Madama Puccini accused the girl of having an affair with the composer. In this particular instance, Ms. Puccini's information was wrong, although her instincts were certainly right.

79 Not particularly, except for maybe Signora Puccini. Puccini had a definite eye for a well-turned ankle, especially when it belonged to someone other than Signora Puccini.

80 At the Metropolitan Opera in New York, on December 10, 1910. The conductor was Arturo Toscanini.

81 *The Hunchback of Notre Dame* by Victor Hugo. He shoulda went with Hugo.

82 *Manon Lescaut.*

83 Pinkerton, Kate and Sharpless in *Madama Butterfly*; everybody in *The Girl of the Golden West* except for Ramerrez, the Mexican bandito.

84 Billy and Wowkle, his politically incorrect squaw.

85 *Il Trittico*, at the Met, on December 14, 1918.

86 Leoncavallo.

87 *Pagliacci*.

88 Paris.

89 The spirits of dead maidens whose lovers forsook them. Hence the phrase "It gives me the willies," i.e., a chill owing to a bad conscience. The Willis turn up in the ballet *Giselle* as well.

90 Medieval Flanders.

91 Ruggero Leoncavallo, of all people.

92 Wagner's *Götterdämmerung*.

93 Alberto Franchetti.

94 In America. The second act would then be in Japan. It probably would have made for a better opera.

95 Emmy Destinn, Enrico Caruso, Pasquale Amato.

96 The Karltheater in Vienna.

97 Robert Moranzoni.

98 *Il tabarro, Suor Angelica, Gianni Schicchi.*

99 Ferruccio Busoni.

100 Wally, Walter and Wanda.

101 Alfredo Catalani.

102 *La Wally.*

103 They all start with the same letter.

104 There is no "w" in Italian.

105 Wanda married Vladimir Horowitz.

106 Horowitz was primarily homosexual.

107 Franco Alfano.

108 Not particularly. Too timid or too respectful to invent his own themes for the opera's closing scene, he worked from Puccini's sketches for the final Turandot-Calaf duet. Then again, his *Turandot* additions are almost always performed in a shortened version with many cuts.

109 *Risurrezione* and *La leggenda di Sakùntala.*

110 At the premiere, he ended the opera where Puccini did, observing, "Here the master lay down his pen." Later, he used the Alfano ending.

111 Yes. The chances that a Puccini opera will get the kind of careful scholarship combined with brilliant musicianship that both Cerha and George Perle have expended on Berg's *Lulu* are slim to none. Besides, if Süssmayr's ending for Mozart's *Requiem* is good enough for us, Alfano is good enough too.

112 Nothing. For a while. Then the Russians came along.

113 Serge Prokofiev and Dmitri Shostakovich, among others.

114 Shostakovich.

115 *Lady Macbeth of Mtsensk*, which was blasted by Stalin in a *Pravda* editorial in January 1936.

116 "Muddle Instead of Music." It sounds worse in Russian, especially when printed in the pages of *Pravda*.

117 Shostakovich never wrote another opera. He did write an operetta in 1939, *The Silly Little Mouse*, which is lost.

118 Considering that *Lady Macbeth* is, to my ears, one of the handful of authentic operatic masterpieces this century has produced, you betcha.

119 *Katarina Ismailova.*

120 It might have been the trombones emulating the sounds of sexual intercourse. Or it might have been something he ate that disagreed with him. Nobody and no thing disagreed with Joe Stalin and got away with it.

121 *The Nose.*

122 Depends on your point of view. Actually, it's far more "modern" than *Lady Macbeth*.

123 False. It's based on a short story by Nicolai Leskov.

124 *The Decembrists* by Yuri Shaporin.

125 Igor Stravinsky.

126 *The Nightingale*, the sketches of which Stravinsky showed to his teacher, Rimsky-Korsakoff, just before the latter's death in 1908.

127 *Mavra.*

128 *Oedipus Rex*, with a libretto by Jean Cocteau; George Enescu's *Oedipe*, Carl Orff's *Oedipus der Tyrann* and Wolfgang Rihm's *Oedipus*.

129 *A Rake's Progress* by William Hogarth. The opera's title substitutes the definite article "the."

130 W.H. Auden and Chester Kallman.

131 The now-defunct Chicago Opera, in 1921. Mary Garden was the company's director and leading soprano.

132 How'd you guess?

133 My little joke! *Knecht Ruprecht* is the German bogeyman, and the title of a famous short piano piece by Schumann. You may resume the quiz now.

134 *Dialogues of the Carmelites* by Francis Poulenc.

135 *L'Enfant et les sortilèges* by Maurice Ravel.

136 Colette.

137 *L'Heure espagnole.*

138 Ralph Vaughn Williams.

139 The Fifth Symphony and *The Pilgrim's Progress.*

140 *The Shepherds of the Delectable Mountains.*

141 *Hugh the Drover.*

142 *Riders to the Sea.*

143 *The Pilgrim's Progress.*

144 *Koanga* by Delius.

145 *Treemonisha* by Scott Joplin.

146 *Paul Bunyan.*

147 *Billy Budd.*

148 *The Turn of the Screw.*

149 *Albert Herring.*

150 *Peter Grimes.*

151 *Curlew River.*

152 *Death in Venice.*

153 *Gloriana.*

154 *The Turn of the Screw.* The line, however, is by Yeats.

155 *Owen Wingrave.*

156 *The Flood*; *Amahl and the Night Visitors.*

157 *Where the Wild Things Are*, written and illustrated by Maurice Sendak.

158 Leoš Janáček, *Jenufa.*

159 *Ariane et Barbe-bleue*, by Dukas, for which Maeterlinck wrote the libretto; *Pélleas et Mélisande* by Debussy, based on the play.

160 *The Markopulos Case*, by Janáček.

161 *Porgy and Bess*, by George Gershwin.

162 Gian Carlo Menotti, in *The Telephone*.

163 Annina, in Menotti's opera of the same name.

164 *Akhnaten*, by Philip Glass.

165 *Bomarzo*, by Alberto Ginastera. It had some naughty bits with a courtesan, memorably portrayed by Joanna Simon, Carly's sister.

166 *Schwanda the Bagpiper*, by Jaromir Weinberger.

167 *La Belle et la Bête*, by Philip Glass.

168 Karlheinz Stockhausen.

169 *Doktor Faustus*, by Giacomo Manzoni.

170 Luciano Berio.

171 It doesn't have anything to do with singing, or even with music. "Opera" is the Latin plural for "Opus" (work), and so it means "works."

That's it—the Fat Lady has sung!

Answers: Savoy-Faire

1 *Thespis.*

2 *HMS Pinafore.*

3 *Patience.*

4 *The Pirates of Penzance.*

5 *Princess Ida.*

6 *The Contrabandista.*

7 *Cox and Box.*

8 *The Mikado.*

9 *Iolanthe.*

10 *The Yeomen of the Guard.*

11 *Ruddigore.*

12 *The Gondoliers.*

13 *Utopia Limited.*

14 *The Grand Duke.*

15 *The Rose of Persia.*

16 *The Emerald Isle.*

Answers: Yet More Name That Tune

1 Berg's *Wozzeck.*

2 Philip Glass's *Satyagraha.*

3 Poulenc's *Les mamelles de Tirésias* (Tiresias's Breasts).

4 Mussorgsky's *Boris Godunov*.

5 Schoenberg's *Moses und Aron*.

6 Strauss's *Elektra*.

Answers: Real People

1 *Nixon in China*, John Adams and Alice Goodman.

2 *La Traviata*, by Verdi.

3 *The Coronation of Poppea*, by Monteverdi.

4 *The Voyage of Edgar Allan Poe*, by Dominick Argento.

5 *Le Cid*, by Massenet.

6 *William Tell*, by Rossini.

7 *Un Ballo in maschera*, by Verdi (original version).

8 *Lulu*, by Alban Berg.

9 *Zar und Zimmermann*, by Albert Lortzing.

10 *The Man Who Mistook His Wife for a Hat*, by Michael Nyman.

11 *The Death of Klinghoffer*, by John Adams and Alice Goodman.

12 *Il Sogno di Scipione*, by Mozart.

13 *Giovanna d'Arco* by Verdi; *The Maid of Orleans* by Tchaikovsky.

14 *Evita* by Andrew Lloyd Webber and Tim Rice.

15 *Lucretia Borgia* by Donizetti.

16 *The Mother of Us All*, by Virgil Thomson.

17 *Satyagraha*, by Philip Glass.

18 *Die Meistersinger*, by Wagner; *Hans Sachs*, by Lortzing.

19 Virgil Thomson again, with *Lord Byron*.

20 *Attila*, by Verdi.

21 *Gloriana*, by Britten; *Elisabetta, regina d'Inghilterra* by Rossini.

22 *The Pilgrim's Progress*, by Ralph Vaughn Williams.

23 *Nabucco*, by Verdi.

24 *Marilyn*, by Ezra Laderman.

25 *Zar und Zimmermann*, by Lortzing.

26 *Guillaume Tell*, by Rossini.

27 *Christophe Columb*, by Darius Milhaud.

28 *Ariane et Barbe-bleue*, by Paul Dukas; *Bluebeard's Castle*, by Bela Bartok.

29 *Tannhäuser.*

30 *Einstein on the Beach*, by Philip Glass and Robert Wilson.

Answers: Who Am I?

1 Adele, in Johann Strauss's *Die Fledermaus.*

2 Elisabeth de Valois in *Don Carlos.*

3 Selika, in Meyerbeer's *L'Africaine.*

4 Gutrune in *Götterdämmerung.*

5 Kundry in *Parsifal.*

6 Lauretta.

7 Rosina Almaviva in *The Marriage of Figaro*, who is (before her marriage to the Count), the ward of Dr. Bartolo. In a way, therefore, she is Figaro's step-sister, since he is Bartolo's illegitimate son.

8 Eva in *Die Meistersinger.*

9 Ellen Orford in Benjamin Britten's *Peter Grimes.*

10 Giulietta in *The Tales of Hoffmann.*

11 Mélisande in Debussy's *Pélleas et Mélisande.*

12 Desdemona in Verdi's *Otello.*

13 Gilda in Verdi's *Rigoletto.*

14 Günther.

15 David in *Die Miestersinger.*

16 Des Grieux in both *Manon Lescaut* and *Manon.*

17 Giorgio Germont in Verdi's *La Traviata.*

18 Masetto.

19 Pimen, Rangoni and Shuisky.

20 John Bunyan.

21 Zinovy in Shostakovich's *Lady Macbeth of Mtsensk.*

22 Sir Edgar in Henze's *Der junge Lord.*

23 Valzacchi in Strauss's *Der Rosenkavalier.*

24 Vasco da Gama in *L'Africaine.*

25 Valentin in Gounod's *Faust.*

26 Basha (Pasha) Selim in *The Abduction from the Seraglio.*

Answers: A + B = C: Musical Equations

1 Alban Berg.

2 W.A. Mozart.

3 Brahms.

4 Wagner.

5 Chopin.

6 Liszt.

7 Verdi.

8 Stravinsky.

9 Berlioz.

10 Mendelssohn.

11 Tchaikovsky.

12 Schubert.

13 Massenet.

14 Puccini.

15 Scott Joplin.

16 Gian Carlo Menotti.

17 Philip Glass.

18 Richard Strauss.

19 Mussorgsky.

20 Arnold Schoenberg.

Answers: Act Three Photo Captions

1 Page 125: Leonard Bernstein.

2 Page 132: Maria Callas left the limelight forever in 1972 with an "around the world in 100 days" series of recitals as a last gift to her admirers.

3 Page 140: Giuseppe di Stefano.

Opposite: Samuel Ramey in *Boris Godunov*

Epilogue

There, that was easy, wasn't it?[1] This brisk trot through operatic history has been designed with one purpose in mind: to make you love and appreciate opera even more than you did when you started.

And how?[2] By expanding your knowledge of the music and librettos—which, after all, are the *sine qua non* of opera. In Hollywood, executives often make fun of the writers; Jack Warner, the legendary chief of Warner Bros., once contemptuously dismissed his writers (some of the best in the business) as "shmucks with Underwoods."[3]

But as an agent I know is fond of saying: "Let them try to make a movie without a writer and see what happens!"[4]

The same is true for opera. What we see up on stage is dazzling: the lavish sets, the ornate costumes, the huge chorus, the glittering stars whose wattage draws us into the theater like the moth to the flame. And what we hear is generally even more wonderful: the glorious sound of the human voice issuing forth from golden throats, the silken textures of the great operatic orchestras led by some of the world's best conductors. It's a feast for both eye and ear, and who can blame anyone for leaving it at that?[5]

You're right: I can. For while it's certainly no sin to attend the opera to show off your new tuxedo or evening gown, to network with business associates, to attend the opera galas and balls, or to hear for yourself whether Signorina Allora is everything the critics say she is, to check out that new conductor everybody's talking about, or to view in person the latest directorial enormity (*Dialogues of the Carmelites* set in a bordello; *Tosca* in 16th-century Portugal) so you can write an angry letter about it to the *New York Times* the next day, there's much more to opera than that.

How much more is what I've tried to show you in this quiz. But a book, of course, can only scratch the surface, can only suggest the rich depth of material that lies beneath the glitter and the glamour of big-time international opera. For while the performers, directors, designers and conductors may get audiences into the tent, it's the composers and scenarists who keep them there, and keep them coming back for more.

Last question: Why do *you* love opera?[6]

Addio!

Answers: Epilogue

1 Maybe, maybe not. But I hope it was fun.

2 I don't know: how?

3 Underwood was a well-known brand of typewriter in the pre-computer era.

4 They already do, you say? Alas, after seeing the latest *Batman* sequel, you might be right!

5 I'll bet you know!

6 That one you'll have to answer for yourself.